Managing and developing HR Careers

Emerging trends and issues

d to the LRC
stamped

Penny Tamkin

Peter Reilly

Wendy Hirsh

The Chartered Institute of Personnel and Development is the leading publisher of books and reports for personnel and training professionals, students, and all those concerned with the effective management of people at work.
For full details of all our titles, please contact the Publishing Department:

Tel.: 020 8612 6204
E-mail: publish@cipd.co.uk

The catalogue of all CIPD titles can be viewed on the CIPD website: www.cipd.co.uk/bookstore

For details of CIPD research projects:
www.cipd.co.uk/research

Managing and developing HR Careers

Emerging trends and issues

Penny Tamkin

Peter Reilly

Wendy Hirsh

Institute for Employment Studies

First published 2006
Reprinted 2006, 2007

Cover design by Curve
Designed by Beacon GDT
Typeset by Paperweight
Printed in Great Britain by Short Run Press, Exeter

British Library Cataloguing in Publication Data:
A catalogue record for this book is available from the British Library

ISBN   1 84398 161 0
ISBN-13 978 1 84398 161 9

Chartered Institute of Personnel and Development
151 The Broadway, London SW19 1JQ
Tel.: 020 8612 6200
E-mail: www.cipd.co.uk
incorporated by Royal Charter: Registered charity no. 1079797.

Contents

Acknowledgements

The CIPD would like to thank the organisations that assisted with this research – Cancer Research UK, Centrica plc, Guy's and St Thomas' NHS Trust, Hays, The Home Office (Immigration and Nationality department), Lovells, The Prudential, and Tameside Metropolitan Authority. We would also like to thank all the people who took part in the research project as survey participants and as interviewees for the case studies, particularly:

◘ Kay Willis, Lovells

◘ Sharron Pamplin, Hays HR Services

◘ Sara Wright and Joe Dugdale, Centrica plc

◘ Deborah Rennie and Martha How, Hewitt Associates

◘ Tim Evans, Cancer Research UK

◘ Russell Martin and Drew.Watson, Prudential UK

◘ Miriam Lawton, Tameside Metropolitan Authority

◘ Terry Coode, Guy's and St Thomas' NHS Trust

◘ John Marsh, The Home Office

We would also like to thank all the HR professionals who gave their time to speak to us about their own career experiences and aspirations.

Foreword

One of the major challenges facing HR is to consider how the function is, and should be, changing, in order to meet modern business challenges. In line with this, the CIPD has committed to exploring 'the changing role and function of HR' as a major research theme over the next few years. As part of this, a series of related research projects are under way to provide up-to-date information about how to organise, skill-up and develop an HR function that is able to deliver high-level performance, and meet the demands of challenging business strategies and changing organisational conditions.

One of the projects that forms part of this investigates the career paths of HR professionals. Major transformations in the workplace in the past few years have resulted in the HR function experiencing considerable change. New HR structures, roles and processes (such as shared service centres, outsourcing and HR business partners) are all thought to have altered career paths for HR professionals in a number of significant ways.

In early 2005, the CIPD commissioned the Institute for Employment Studies (IES) to work on the project with the following aims:

◘ To gain a clear view of the most common career paths for HR professionals (specialists and generalists).

◘ To understand how career paths are changing as new roles and structures appear.

◘ To obtain views on the most successful routes to the top positions in HR as well as the critical skills, qualifications, experiences and attributes that are needed to succeed.

◘ To uncover the career aspirations of HR professionals and reasons for a choice of HR as a career.

◘ To clarify how organisations explicitly manage and develop HR careers and, if so, what career path models and career development activities, including the provision of career advice, are currently being used most successfully.

When starting this research, the CIPD's assumption was that new structures and processes in HR were altering career paths in a fundamental way, but that there was uncertainty over whether this was a feature solely of large, complex organisations or something that was happening more widely. Changing HR roles – for example, the creation of business partners – may be affecting the sort of staff seeking to move into HR; while the pressure on HR to be attuned to business needs may result in more people heading out of the function during their careers to gain this experience. Specialist roles in HR are growing, but does this mean that there are distinct career paths for this group, independent of those for generalists? And what is the impact of shared service centres and outsourcing on career paths for HR professionals? Finally, there is the perceived need for HR to develop new skills to meet the challenges of tomorrow's organisation.

This research sought to gain some initial answers to these questions and to build understanding of the nature and shape of HR careers today.

The CIPD's (2003) *Managing Employee Careers* survey reported renewed interest in the area of career management, but a key finding was that organisational career support activities were often considered ineffective. Providing career support to employees was often seen as a 'nice to have' rather than an essential activity. The question that arises is whether this is true for those in the HR function. Are they receiving fairly limited career advice and support? And how is professional development being treated alongside general development activities? Given the widespread changes to HR structures and roles, how are organisations responding in terms of the provision of learning and career development opportunities they offer their HR professionals?

The research project has used a mixture of methods to investigate experiences and perceptions of careers in HR:

- a review of existing literature and research on career paths in general and in relation to HR specifically

- a survey of approximately 1,800 HR practitioners (CIPD, 2005)

- nine case studies that looked at how organisations are managing and developing the careers of their HR professionals. The case studies were chosen to reflect sector, size and location to give different perspectives on HR careers.

We hope the research will be helpful to CIPD members at all stages in their careers. In particular, we hope that it will assist members in navigating and developing their careers, as well as helping those who are responsible for the development of staff in the function. The report summarises all this material, but the full description of the 2005 survey results can be found on the CIPD website at www.cipd.co.uk/surveys and the detailed case studies at www.cipd.co.uk/hrcareerpaths.

Jessica Jarvis
CIPD Adviser, Learning, Training and Development
jessica.jarvis@cipd.co.uk

Executive summary

Major transformations in the workplace in the past few years have resulted in the HR function experiencing considerable change. New HR structures, roles and processes such as shared service centres, outsourcing and HR business partners are thought to have altered career paths in a fundamental way. This research aimed to find out the extent to which this was happening, and to identify the implications for HR professionals aiming to carve out their own careers as well as organisations trying to manage and develop the careers of their HR teams.

This report details the findings from a review of the literature examining changes to the HR function and HR careers, a survey of approximately 1,800 HR practitioners about their careers and nine in-depth organisational case studies looking at how organisations are managing and developing the careers of their HR professionals.

What has emerged from this research is a range of potential tensions for the function that revolve around roles in HR and the consequent changing shape of HR careers. Underpinning these tensions is the fact that, in many organisations, the function has fundamentally changed its interaction with the organisation. New forms of organisation driven by a philosophy of greater consolidation, standardisation and automation have resulted in many HR functions seeking to shift their emphasis from administration and operational matters to strategic partnership and change management.

Demarcations between transactional and 'transformational' activities have always existed, but are now more marked than ever. Similar traditional distinctions between specialists and generalists are also becoming more emphasised, especially in large organisations where there are centres of expertise and business partners. These

distinct HR communities can sometimes become quite separated in location, leadership, philosophy, aims and stakeholder interactions, and these divisions may mean that ideas, approaches, views and talent are not shared. The fact that skill requirements are also different makes the task of developing people into these roles all the harder.

For those within the HR function the message is that, within some organisations and across the HR community as a whole, fragmented career paths are arising from the separation of service centres, centres of expertise and business partners. In future people will have to make 'zigzag' moves to gain operational experience, close working with the business and expert know-how in key disciplines of HR.

Just how has HR responded? From this research it would seem that the initial focus has been on redesigning roles and structures in HR to reflect the three-legged model of Ulrich and others. The findings also indicate that, in some cases, there has, in fact, been too much focus on that and not enough attention paid to other aspects intimately connected to making a success of such restructure and role changes. These complementary changes are to skills, processes and career paths. HR needs to pay more attention to these key areas if it is to nurture and retain talent.

The brightest and best are finding HR a difficult nut to crack. Graduates are selecting HR as a potential career but then finding their experiences are not greatly valued, and the jobs available to them are few in number and often dull. Getting in is bad enough, but moving on can be even more fraught. Entry-level jobs, designed as such and with progression and development opportunities built in, are rare. Alongside this, traditional routes in for those keen on the administrative side of personnel are also less easy to access and many felt these were drying up. The function needs to think carefully about where new entrants fit and how they progress. Deliberate developmental roles for HR graduates and other entrants would be much welcomed.

Changing job roles means changing skill sets and there is a general view emerging from this research that some skill sets are hard to find. OD (organisational development) roles, where technical and consultancy knowledge, skills and experience are combined, are problematic to resource and organisations also find business partner roles difficult to fill. This is, perhaps, not surprising, as traditional HR hierarchies have not created enough people ready for these newly emerging career streams.

The HR function usually holds responsibility for career development policy in the organisation, but is the function practising what it preaches when it comes to the career development of its own people? This study shows a very mixed picture. Overall career development was patchy, with the majority of case-study organisations feeling that they should have rather more systematic approaches to developing careers, but lacking these at present. Overall, it seems that a gap is emerging between the aspirations of the function to deliver certain roles and its ability to develop individuals into them. In the future, active management of careers will become increasingly necessary if the moves from specialist to generalist and between the various parts of the HR function are to become a reality.

1 | Changing careers in the 'new' HR function

Before looking at overall trends in organisational careers, it is helpful to review the context in which careers are being developed. In particular, there is a need to consider structural and process change, including to what degree HR activities have been outsourced. In addition, the relationship between HR and line management is discussed. These developments have affected the size and shape of the function; the roles it plays and tasks it undertakes. This necessarily impacts upon the number and nature of HR jobs and the relationships between them.

These changes are likely to have been greater for those employed in large, complex organisations (in both the public and private sectors), where structural and process reform has been more extensive. For small HR teams, there may have been both less change in structures and hence in options for career development.

The new HR function

Changes to organisational structures

Recent research (eg CIPD, 2003; Reilly and Williams, 2003) has shown that many large HR functions have now moved to a 'three-legged' functional design, often associated with the work of Dave Ulrich (1995), with a central shared service centre, business partners and centres of expertise (see Figure 1, below). This has replaced integrated HR teams that carry out the full range of HR activities from administration to strategic direction. Prior to this, large organisations frequently had separate HR teams, doing largely the same thing, to reflect differences in geography, business unit or, sometimes, grade. Each location, department or grade grouping might have had its own team. The only debate was about the

Figure 1 | A new model of HR

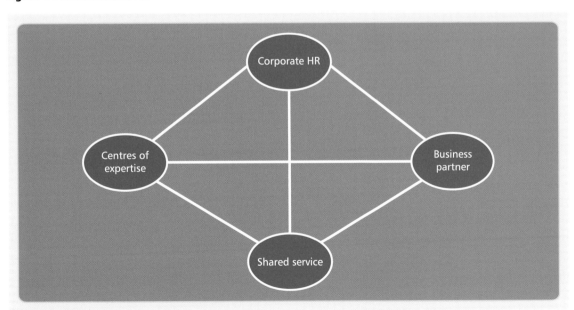

> 'In practice, as many shared service operations have been introduced as a cost-saving measure, they have taken on more the form of centralisation than customisation of services.'

extent of delegated authority. In other words, how centralised or decentralised the decision-making was.

In shared services, activities performed locally by divisions or business units are re-engineered, streamlined and centralised, so that the various business units pool resources and 'share' in the service delivery solution. So, there is a common provision of services with (in theory) the nature of the services determined primarily by the customer. In practice, as many shared service operations have been introduced as a cost-saving measure, they have taken on more the form of centralisation than customisation of services (Reilly and Williams, 2003). HR shared services covers a wide variety of activities, the principal components of which are usually the undertaking of administrative tasks, and the provision of information and advice through intranets and call centres. Some companies add consultancy or project support from a shared service centre. Recruitment to the new jobs in the shared service function (especially the customer-facing ones) has been from non-HR as well as HR resource pools. Those with good interpersonal skills and customer handling experience have been particularly valued, even over those with prior HR knowledge.

Nearly all large organisations now have HR personnel in key business relationship roles, generally described as business partners. The latter either report to a senior line manager or to a senior HR manager. These individuals, or at most small teams (sometimes with some internal consultancy capacity), are expected to support their line clients in strategic development, organisational design and change management. The person in this role normally also brokers the delivery of transactional services from the shared services operation and acts as the conduit with corporate HR. The emphasis on business

knowledge suggests that these roles may be filled from those outside the function. Experience to date suggests that organisations find it difficult to locate candidates who can offer both HR and business know-how (Reilly and Williams, forthcoming; Lawler, Mueller-Oerlinghausen and Shearn, 2005).

Centres of expertise with capability in such areas as resourcing, employee relations, reward and training give professional support to business partners, often developing detailed policy for corporate HR and acting as a reference point for shared services agents dealing with complex issues raised by clients. Professional HR experience is more in demand for these specialist posts.

Corporate HR, often a small team, is usually responsible for the strategic direction of the function, with a broad policy overview. A governance role is nearly always included, meaning that the organisation should continue to adhere to certain standards and follow the same broad approach to people management. Senior management issues (pay and succession) might also be reserved for the corporate centre, along with external affairs. Again, professional HR experience is valued at the corporate centre of HR, but, such is the desire for business alignment, senior appointments may also come from outside the function.

The expectation at the outset of this research was that career paths today would be different from those in the past and in general would be more restricted. The traditional functional model (shown in Figure 2, opposite) allowed movement vertically up the departmental pyramid.

Today, career progression will either be more difficult or more crab-like, as segmentation between the roles deepens (see Figure 3, opposite).

Figure 2 | Traditional career structure

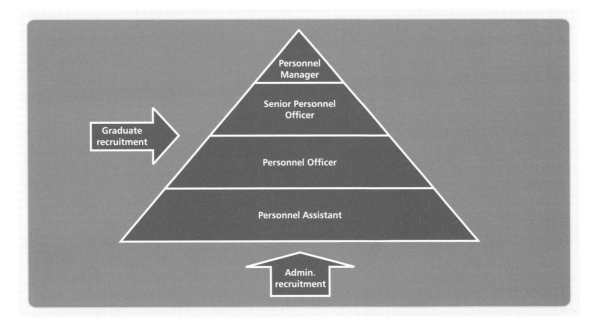

Figure 3 | Possible HR career map in new model

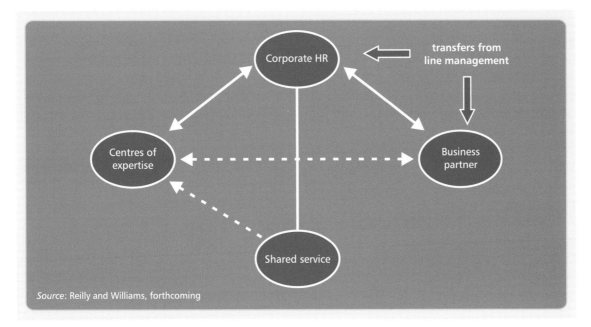

> 'Manager self-service and employee self-service are continuing to eliminate tasks previously performed by HR staff.'

It will be hard, as companies are already reporting, for those in shared services roles to move straight to business partner positions – the jump from transactional to transformational work is just too large. It may be easier to move from shared services to centres of expertise, because there is not the requirement to operate in such a strategic or business-focused role. However, deep knowledge will still have to be acquired somehow. Corporate HR will be able to source posts from both centres of expertise and business partner roles and send staff in the opposite direction. The emerging view in some organisations is that traffic between business partner and centres of expertise may be one-way. Business partners may be able to develop specialist knowledge (to add to their business know-how), but the experts in training and development, reward or employee relations may find it hard to grow into change agents, as opposed to advisers, unless there is a specialist OD function.

Issues that arise from the segmentation of the HR function are beyond the scope of this report. However, they do have implications for career paths. It seems that many organisations have put structural and process change in place before tackling skills or careers (Reilly and Williams, forthcoming). As a result, it is only now that attention is being given to career management – as some of the case studies will show. Various strategies are being implemented, from creating short-term development opportunities (eg through temporary assignments) to more structural adjustments (eg creating new roles or changing reporting relationships).

Process change and e-HR

Another change to the operational context for many more sophisticated organisations is the simplification of processes combined with greater automation. Manager self-service and employee self-service are continuing to eliminate tasks previously performed by HR staff. Self-service has moved from the static display of information on an organisation's intranet to individual access to personal data with the ability to modify or update their HR records. Manager self-service has gone beyond transactional processes to decision-making relating to reward, performance management and resourcing.

In parallel, some service delivery tasks have also been significantly transformed by technology. Recruitment and training are two of the most popular areas of development. Much of the front end of the recruitment process, for example, has been automated, relieving HR of much tedious administration, but also some selection (really sifting) activities. HR's role has progressively shifted in organisations applying e-HR from processing data to designing intranets, populating them with intelligible information and introducing protocols to facilitate self-managed systems.

Progress on e-HR naturally varies by size and sector of organisation. Cost is an impediment for many organisations in proceeding along these lines. Nonetheless, the new generation of HR Information Systems (HRIS) do facilitate self-service solutions. Much of the cost reduction in the public sector is predicated on the introduction of e-HR and it has been a key feature of process re-engineering in big private sector firms.

As far as careers are concerned, the more tasks that are automated, the fewer administrative roles there will be. This should also upskill those performing these jobs. The result may be that the flow into more senior HR posts is reduced, but the

> **'Outsourcing, where it occurs, is generally tactical, not strategic, in nature; focused on specific activities.'**

quality is enhanced. Others in HR, in theory, should have more time to undertake more strategic activities in support of the business. Evidence from the USA suggests that this transformational expectation is yet to be realised (Lawler and Mohrman, 2003).

The impact of HR outsourcing

There have been some well-publicised major HR outsourcing deals, such as those involving BT, BP, BAe Systems, Boots and Westminster Council. In these organisations significant chunks of HR activity, principally involving administrative tasks, have been outsourced. Clearly, in these organisations career paths are not what they were (see Figure 4, below). There is no feed-in from below of those undertaking clerical, administrative and call centre/help desk roles. Most of the positions require professional or business expertise. So hiring or transfers will happen at these levels.

However, those organisations that have removed their support activities entirely are very much the exception. Outsourcing, where it occurs, is generally tactical, not strategic, in nature; focused on specific activities. Thus training administration may have been contracted out, but not training delivery. HR careers in these organisations will not be as straightforward as in the past, but there remains the possibility of vertical career development: from personnel assistant to personnel manager.

Devolvement to line managers

There has been a move for some time now towards managers becoming more self-reliant and taking on a wider range of responsibilities and decision-making in the area of people management. The reasoning has been to strip out bureaucracy and produce faster decision-making through increasing local accountability and to give HR time to play a more strategic role

Figure 4 | HR career map with outsourced administration

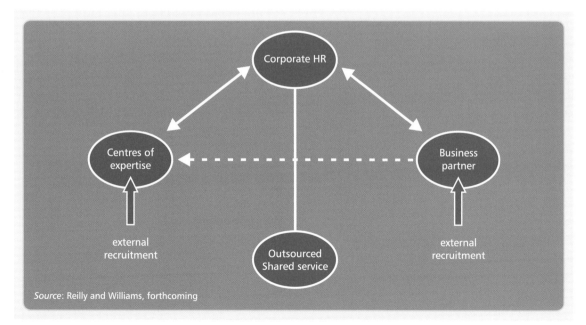

Source: Reilly and Williams, forthcoming

In practice, what has been devolved has varied greatly from organisation to organisation. In general, policy direction and process design remain with HR, but many practical people-management tasks are now undertaken by line management. Research by Torrington (1998) suggests that on some subjects it is more common for management to develop strategy without HR participation (especially work design), whereas on others HR may take a stronger lead (eg recruitment). However, on the vast majority of subjects there is a clear line/HR partnership at work (namely, on HR planning, performance management, training, management development, career management, employee relations and reward).

Despite the opportunities e-HR presents, more up-to-date evidence suggests that the devolvement position is relatively unchanged. The line and HR continue in partnership over people management. According to a CIPD survey in 2004, half of organisations reported that recruitment and selection is shared against, in nearly a third, the line in control (CIPD, 2004). By contrast, although employee relations is shared in 40 per cent of companies, in half HR takes the lead. Reward is more HR biased; training and development more shared.

The impact on the HR function, in those organisations where the changes noted above have occurred, has been to reduce its size and re-position it so that it gets away from its 'nanny' role and from low-level tasks to higher value-added, strategic activities. This direction of travel is consistent with the aims of standardisation, automation and consolidation that underpin shared services, e-HR and with process redesign.

General trends in careers

Having reviewed changes to the HR function in recent years, we will now examine current trends in relation to 'careers' and how career development occurs in employing organisations. We will start with some of the high-level debates about the existence or demise of careers and go on to the more specific career issues of professional groups in the workforce.

Traditional versus flexible careers

Over the past 15 years or so, much of the debate about careers and career paths has been dominated by the question of whether traditional or bureaucratic career paths are being replaced by more fluid and unpredictable careers.

The twin drivers for a change in the nature of careers are normally taken to be technological change and global competition. These are seen as pushing large employers towards more flexible work organisation with more outsourcing to smaller firms and self-employed people and an increased use of part-time and temporary workers (Castells, 1996; Atkinson and Meager, 1986). 'Flatter structures' are also assumed to be reducing opportunities for upward career progression through promotion.

These changes have obvious implications for career paths and career management, as discussed by Collin and Watts (1996). Jarvis (2003) argues for a 'paradigm shift' in our thinking about careers, based on the need for career management skills within an increasingly flexible labour market characterised by project-based work, insecurity and changing skill requirements. Arthur and Rousseau (1996) describe the 'boundaryless career' in which an individual moves much more freely across organisational boundaries. Kanter (1989) sees professional or entrepreneurial careers as growing in importance in the knowledge economy. Handy (1994) popularised the idea of the 'portfolio' career, in which an individual would conduct work of various kinds in various ways rather than be a full-time employee of a single organisation. Bridges (1994) was more extreme and predicted the demise of 'the job' as well as of organisational careers in an increasingly chaotic market for work.

The validity of a major 'paradigm shift' in the nature of careers has been questioned by many writers including the Trades Union Congress (2000), Bradley *et al* (2000) and Nolan (2003). These and other researchers have looked to labour market data to see if the world of work is really changing fundamentally. For example, job tenure was largely stable in the period 1975 to the mid-1990s (Gregg and Wadsworth, 1999) and has only fallen very modestly since (Macauley, 2003). The major ESRC-funded programme on the 'Future of Work' has concluded that much of the rhetoric of the end of the organisational career is not supported by labour-market evidence (Taylor, 2004; White *et al*, 2004). Two interesting items noted in the workplace survey were the re-introduction of organisational levels ('relayering'), and the increasing proportion of employees who feel their best chance of improving their prospects is to stay with their current employers (comparing 1990 with 2000). So career opportunities within employing organisations have not disappeared as was predicted.

Non-standard employment (part-time work, temporary work and self-employment) has not been growing quickly in the UK, and recent

research shows that such patterns are concentrated in those at the very early stages and those at the end of their careers (Weir, 2003; Felstead *et al*, 1999). We were interested to see in this research whether self-employment, for example, is seen as a career option mainly by HR people towards the end of their careers or at all career stages.

Corporately-managed or self-managed careers

Against a backcloth of uncertainty about careers in large organisations, the dominant trend has been for major employers in the UK to pass more of the responsibility for career development to the employee, albeit with line managers being exhorted to offer support (Hirsh and Jackson, 2004; CIPD, 2003). Many writers would argue it is necessary and healthy for all workers, including employees in large organisations, to develop what Waterman *et al* (1994) called 'career resilience.'

However, a reverse trend has been operating in respect of employees seen as 'talented' or 'high-potential'. The late 1990s saw a resurgence of interest in getting and retaining the very best quality employees, especially those with leadership potential in the so-called 'war for talent' (Chambers *et al*, 1998). We therefore see considerable effort going into the proactive career development of potential leaders (Hirsh, 2003) and especially in facilitating career paths which give wider career experience by crossing functional or business unit boundaries. We also see the continuing use of high-potential graduate entry programmes as a means of attracting high-quality graduates and giving them planned early career experience (Barber *et al*, 2005). This study showed less conscious corporate attention is being paid to good graduates who enter large organisations in

> **'More and more organisations are realising that specialists do need many of the wider skills associated with management and leadership.'**

specific jobs (often at low levels) but who have potential for further career progression. As one suspects, many young HR professionals might fall into this category, and we were, therefore, interested to see whether those involved in this study felt that they receive positive career development support from their local managers or the HR function.

Recent research on the links between HRM and high-performing organisations shows that positive career development is one mechanism for increasing employee engagement and motivation, so the downplaying of organisational careers for the majority of employees may not be a wise strategy (Purcell et al, 2003).

The careers of specialists and professionals

There is a large literature on the career paths and employment needs of professionals and people in specialist or technical roles. These issues have been explored for over 50 years and the messages are remarkably consistent. As the majority of people in HR might see themselves as pursuing a professional career, and a significant number might see themselves as 'specialists', we might expect some of these themes to be evident in the empirical data collected in this study.

Dalton et al, (1977) proposed a model of four stages of specialist careers, based on a study of professionals working in the US. The four stages of increasing contribution are apprenticeship, independence, mentoring and strategic. Dalton (1989) found that significant numbers of professionals at level three hold specialist roles with little or no management responsibility, but that many will not get beyond level two (independence), especially if they do not have wider skills.

Arnold (1997) gives a helpful overview of some of the issues concerning separate career paths or ladders for specialists. He proposes that, in modern organisations, separating managerial and professional work into different jobs done by different kinds of people is not at all straightforward. Grady and Fineham (1990) are among those calling for dual career paths for scientists and managers with 'equal opportunities for status and compensation'.

More and more organisations are realising that specialists do need many of the wider skills associated with management and leadership. As a result, some researchers have emphasised the need to recruit technical people with good interpersonal skills and a commercial orientation, and to develop project management skills (Grady and Fineham, 1990).

Specialist careers do not just have to meet the distinct needs that organisations have for specialists. They may need to be geared to the particular career interests and aspirations of the individuals who choose specialised work.

Arnold (1997) reviewed the evidence on the 'special needs' of specialists and demonstrated that 'job challenge' matters a great deal to people who choose to pursue specialist work as the main feature of their careers. In other words, it is the work itself – and especially how demanding and interesting it is – that really matters. Arnold finds the evidence on the importance of working conditions less conclusive. On balance, intrinsic rewards seem more important than extrinsic ones.

Hoppe (1993) looked at the work goals of international research and development scientists. The top four were challenge, freedom, a good relationship with their manager and co-operation. The lowest were working for a prestigious organisation, employment security, and good physical working conditions.

One might expect that specialists need little management, being very skilled people. However, the literature challenges this view. A collection of useful, largely American, books, looks at the particular challenges of managing professionals – mostly in scientific or professional service firms. McKenna and Maister (2002), in their book *First Among Equals*, highlight the dangers of under-managing professionals who may 'do their own thing' and pay insufficient attention to the needs of the organisation as a whole. However, over-managing them is equally deadly, as their enthusiasm and creativity can easily be crushed by over-control. The senior specialist may be highly skilled, but may often be thin-skinned. They see encouragement as the key to managing specialists effectively, plus individualised attention to career and development issues. According to IES research, 'underpinning the successful management of knowledge workers is trust; such workers need to have control over their knowledge and how they apply it, and management must be tolerant of risk-taking' (Suff and Reilly, 2005).

Recent CIPD work, *Managing the Careers of Professional Knowledge Workers* (Swart and Kinnie, 2005) emphasises the multiple work identities held by professionals, and the high value they place on their own career development. These themes of professional identity, the need for good management and the crucial importance of positive career development have been found in so many studies of knowledge workers that we must assume they are very likely to apply to specialist HR professionals as well.

Career paths in HR

In a study of the careers of a number of corporate support functions, Lambert (2002) found that breadth within such functions was important to career progression. This study also drew attention to the importance of 'specialisms' of HR work (employee relations, reward, learning and development etc) both in defining a broad range of know-how falling within HR, and offering differing degrees of specialist career progression. The research also examined a long-running interest in whether HR directors come from the HR profession or from other backgrounds. In the major organisations participating in this research, it is still quite common for HR Directors to be from functions other than HR. This is rarely the case for finance directors. For example, Bates (2001) cited a survey of 53 top US companies showing that about a quarter of senior HR professionals came into their positions without a background in HR.

Research examining the training and development function (Carter *et al*, 2002) showed significant change and evolution in the role of the function in many organisations. Although mostly still regarded as a sub-function of HR, the work of people in this area is demanding new skills, especially in the learning process, but also in business understanding and a range of professional skills (from the use of ICT, to business partner skills, to coaching and counselling and contract management).

IRS (2004) carried out a survey of the careers of 135 top HR professionals in UK organisations in both public and private sectors. Although a comparatively small sample, it is worth noting some of the results:

◻ Reasons for entering HR as a career path included wanting to work with people (41 per cent), attractive career proposition (36 per cent), natural progression (32 per cent) and 27 per cent had entered HR careers by chance.

◘ These HR leaders did feel that having a background in HR and business experience were both important, but attached less importance to having a professional qualification. Only 14 per cent felt that a lack of professional qualification in HR was a barrier to career progression once employed in HR, although 26 per cent saw it as a barrier to entering HR.

◘ A number of barriers to career progression were noted, including a lack of senior HR opportunities (59 per cent), HR not viewed as important enough by employers (49 per cent) and progression limited by a lack of HR strategy (47 per cent). Gender and age discrimination were also factors noted by over one-fifth of the sample.

Weekes (2005) suggests considerable 'sector hopping' by HR executives as a means of securing career progression. In a much wider study of the careers of managers and professionals, Nicholson and West (1988) found many made 'outspiralling' career moves – moving up a level by changing organisation – especially when they felt blocked in their own organisation. These moves were especially common among women.

Issues highlighted by the literature

This brief overview of the literature on the HR function, careers and career paths in HR, highlights a number of emerging issues that this project aims to examine in more depth:

◘ The potential impact of the changing nature and structure of the HR function within organisations on the careers of HR people. In particular, the effect that the arrival of shared services, business partners and centres of expertise have had on career paths, especially where new structures have been accompanied by outsourcing, devolvement of work to line managers, process re-engineering and e-HR.

◘ The extent to which organisational and social change is leading personnel people to feel that they are pursuing flexible rather than conventional careers. We might expect to see this in attitudes to self-employment, willingness to work in small organisations and in consultancy, and in the priority accorded to work–life balance issues.

◘ Whether personnel professionals pursuing specialist career paths have the career attitudes typical of other groups of specialist professionals – a high degree of affiliation to their profession rather than to their employer and sensitivity to intrinsic rewards and personal support from their managers.

◘ The balance for HR professionals between being left to manage their own careers and being pro-actively supported by their employers in their career development.

◘ The nature of skills and experience required for those pursuing a career in HR, and whether, indeed, HR represents one broad career or a number of increasingly specialist sub-careers (eg in areas such as reward or learning and development).

◘ If HR presents diverse areas of experience, then one might expect career paths to be 'zigzag' in nature not just straightforward ladders. But what kinds of moves are important to make? These might be moves between organisations, or between areas of HR or between HR and other business functions.

◘ Whether the careers of those achieving senior leadership positions (eg HR Directors) are rather different from the majority of HR people. In particular, how much prior experience of HR do HR Directors need? How do they best combine professional expertise with wider business and leadership credibility?

2 | Getting into HR

Inevitably, the very beginning of an HR career (or any career of choosing) is a mix of aspiration, practicality and reality. We were interested in finding out what it is that brings people into the function (ie what is attractive about the function from the outside), as well as looking at the process of engagement and the steps people take to begin their HR career path.

The attraction of HR

People are drawn towards the function by some powerful attractants that inevitably differ by position and role in the organisation. From the interviews undertaken as part of this research, it seems that for more senior people and specialists:

◘ HR is seen positively as a key organisational hub, working with a range of business functions and internal customers and having an unrivalled overview of the organisation.

◘ HR provides a workload which is potentially challenging and constantly changing.

◘ HR nestles in the centre of the organisation, close to the political heart and therefore, it offers all that is associated with organisational politics, interest and influence.

Other views were more frequently (but not exclusively) voiced by those in more junior roles:

◘ Wanting to work with people is a hackneyed term and one that several admitted they found slightly embarrassing, yet, for many, it is still a reason why the function appeals.

◘ Making a difference to people's work lives though the operation of an effective and efficient service, and making a difference to the organisation.

◘ And for all levels of staff, the increasing professionalism and credibility of the function raises its appeal to a better-qualified intake.

These views would appear to support the conclusions of Arnold (1997) that job challenge is a major motivator for specialists – it is the perceived nature of the work of HR which people are interested in. It is also consistent with IRS's survey result that 41 per cent of the sample wanted to work with people (IRS, 2004).

Starting the journey

The attraction of the function is one thing, but the means by which individuals make their journey into HR is quite another. Perhaps the most surprising finding of this research is the frequency of an accidental entry into HR. Although, one should not be completely surprised, given the IRS survey finding that 27 per cent had entered HR careers by chance. In our case studies, luck or accident seem to predominate. This is far removed from the expectation that a profession should be purposefully chosen. The question arises, of course, as to whether this is different for other professions or career paths. We would suspect that the most established professions are likely to be defined by more deliberate entry – they rely on long and specific training and post-training work experience, but this might be contrasted with newer professions and more flexible options.

A common theme at the **Home Office** was that, for the majority of interviewees, they had somehow fallen into HR from very different career paths. For a very few, HR was a more deliberative career choice, in one case involving a CIPD professional development scheme and quickly specialising in reward and employee relations. A relative newcomer had identified HR as an area of interest as part of a business studies degree.

> '**Some respondents (around one-third of our interviewees) saw HR as their career of choice and made a substantial effort to engage with it …**'

Some respondents (around one-third of our interviewees) saw HR as their career of choice and made a substantial effort to engage with it, identifying and studying relevant degrees or carefully weighing up career options and plumping for HR. Younger graduates had the chance of studying business degrees and opting for specialisation in HR. HR becomes an increasingly favoured option as people progress through their degree. This choice came about particularly through an enjoyable experience on placements – ie for positive reasons that it is the most interesting option. The decision was also sometimes made for less positive reasons – marketing is over subscribed and competition for jobs is fierce; finance is dull!

I did an HND in business studies, followed by a one year IPD course. I chose HR because I enjoyed that area the most in my HND course. My first job was as a graduate trainee at Courage. This gave me great experience, but little accountability.

HR was the best choice in a business studies degree. Finance was boring, marketing over-subscribed and the people part the most interesting.

Changing entry routes

An entry route into HR via administration was a common avenue in the past. Typically, those who had followed this entry stream would have been a general administrator who subsequently took on some degree of responsibility for staffing. This shift revealed an interest or aptitude for a people-focused role that led to a progressive move in this direction. This was often followed by the pursuit of a professional CIPD qualification.

In **Cancer Research UK**, some non-HR jobs in the organisation provide an entry point into HR work. In the

retail part of the organisation it is possible for people who know the nature of the work in the shops to move into a training role without necessarily having a background in training or HR. The central development and training roles are filled by people with specialist knowledge of this area. Some of the work in Resourcing also provides opportunity for 'first jobbers' in HR, as does the Service Centre.

In the **Prudential**, the Bristol shared service centre ('Ask HR') is now an entry point into HR for people with a customer service or relationship management background. Employees who have done fairly general office work can move into HR via this route and receive training on-the-job. Among those who were currently doing specialist and business partner roles, early career access to HR has quite often been through administrative or support roles. This was this case even for recent entrants to HR with relevant degrees in business, psychology etc.

In **Tameside Council**, individuals traditionally come into the function from administration, they get the opportunity to study for CIPD and then become an HR adviser, but the authority finds few who aspire to senior roles. Our focus group interviewees reflected this entry stream, with most having entered the authority as a junior entrant and making the choice with regard to personnel at an early stage. Some concern was expressed that this stream may be less available in the future as the creation of an HR support team, which focuses on the administrative role and is more isolated from the HR advisers, will make the move more difficult.

There were also those whose preferred career was in something quite different but which, for a range of reasons, did not progress in practice. Qualified chemists, professional musicians, aspiring social workers, all by some twist of fate 'fell into' the function and settled there.

At **Hewitts**, although HR Operations has a number of long-serving staff, there has been a fair amount of recent external recruitment of HR practitioners, too. Three people had experience of people management as students that led them into HR. Three interviewees arrived in people management work via other disciplines, as diverse as technical writing, accountancy and social security administration. They stayed in the people management field because they found the work interesting.

At **Guy's and St Thomas'** there had been shifts in resourcing practices. It was felt that a lot of people had come up through the ranks in the past but, increasingly, the organisation demanded good qualifications for entry-level jobs and, therefore, more people are graduates and some have master's degrees. There were several comments on the difficulty of breaking into the HR profession, new CIPD graduates start at the bottom and spend a long time in the trust before they touch anything of any significance. One interviewee commented that new degree courses specialising in HR would increasingly form a route into the function.

Our younger HR interviewees had often joined the function through quite different routes from their older peers. The changing nature of the HR profession has meant that new routes have appeared as old routes have diminished in importance. Coming into HR through a business studies degree is a relatively new stream and has its own dynamic.

The views of those who had joined HR through a related degree subject was that the function was not only difficult to enter but also difficult to find a role which adds anything of any value in a reasonable timescale.

In the **Home Office** there were three visible career streams:

- There were those who were generic administrators first and foremost and who now work within HR, but with considerable generic skills and overlap of role with other administrators across the organisation.

- There were those who had entered the function from other parts of the department as part of a civil service career.

- Qualified HR professionals who had come into the Home Office from other organisations.

There was a view that in the past many people had 'ended up' in HR without an HR background or HR qualifications but that now there were two key trends visible. First, it now feels as if entry is a more conscious career choice and second, there has been a process of upskilling with an increasing number of graduates in the function.

At **Cancer Research UK**, most of the focus group members were still early in their careers and had taken quite diverse routes into HR. One of the striking features of this group was that they were highly qualified (most were graduates, quite often in related disciplines such as business or psychology), but they had found it quite difficult to gain entry to a career in HR. Several had taken quite low-level office jobs and come in through admin in the HR function (a filing clerk at a bank, in one case). Some commented on the lack of graduate entry places in HR – several had tried going for corporate graduate entry schemes but failed to get recruited this way.

A big 'catch-22' in early career is that most organisations ask for at least two years' experience plus a CIPD qualification for HR advisers. However, it is difficult to find an employer to support CIPD training and to help with its costs. So HR assistants have to move around at this level for a while until they find an employer wishing to support their CIPD training and develop them towards adviser-level work. One of the participants had taken a

> 'Line managers can add value with a different perspective and help to ground the function within the operational reality of the organisation, but they also need to acknowledge their lack of expertise.'

sandwich degree which also gave her the CIPD qualification – others felt this type of accreditation would make professional entry much easier.

Some people enter HR work in mid-career from a background in general or operational management:

I took a Master's in HR when I was still working in general management. I was doing a lot of people management and was intrigued by it. At the time I saw the master's programme as learning about what I was already doing. Now I see a bigger cultural difference between HR and general management to do with taking a systems and process view of people.

More senior roles are often filled by direct recruitment of people with significant HR experience in varied sectors.

Several people we interviewed had begun their careers in very different professions and organisations or from general clerical roles.

I trained as a secretary but the pay was not very good and, after a series of career changes, I moved to British Rail as a clerical officer. In 1988 I was providing an admin service, including payroll for the depot, and was promoted. As my job became more personnel-focused I did the CIPD through BR which had great (training) systems and processes.

Passing through

These previous examples assume a career choice of HR or, at least, a happy accident that people settle with. Of course, there are those who do not necessarily intend to remain in the function (although they were a minority among those we

interviewed). This includes line managers, who see a spell in HR as adding value to their own development and, indeed, to the function itself. In approximately half our case studies, we spoke to individuals who had entered the function from line management roles. This route is relatively common in the Civil Service, although an increased move to professionalisation may diminish this flow. Here, the deal is to bring and take knowledge, skills and perspectives in a mutually beneficial way. The challenge is to be able to do so while negotiating the increasing professionalisation of the function. Line managers can add value with a different perspective and help to ground the function within the operational reality of the organisation, but they also need to acknowledge their lack of expertise. HR colleagues need to be supportive so that the individual can integrate comfortably, without becoming exposed. It is more likely that line managers will be successful in generalist, rather than specialist, posts, since for the latter they may lack the necessary knowledge, skills and experience. The exception to this rule, we understand, might be in learning and development, where business awareness could be particularly helpful.

In **Hewitts**, the advantage of line management experience was seen to be the ability to see issues from the business perspective. This helped when dealing with business leaders and may help complement what internal HR offers.

Having done both specialist and generalist roles within HR in the same organisation, I took a move into a line management role in the sales area for several years. I went for this because I reached the top of the HR career ladder in my part of the

> **'Graduate entry is becoming more commonplace and more desirable although, as we have seen, the quality of jobs available to new graduate entrants has been criticised.'**

country, and because the regional director encouraged me. Having profit and loss responsibility for 90 people was great commercial learning, and dealing with people issues as a line manager added very much to my personal maturity. I then moved back into HR into a regional director position. Our talent processes are now trying to help these kinds of moves – which need some pushing – to happen. Our CEO sees value in moving good people between functions.

The organisational perspective

From an organisational perspective, entry streams into HR are seen to be changing, with a move away from the traditional administration routes of the past. Graduate entry is becoming more commonplace and more desirable although, as we have seen, the quality of jobs available to new graduate entrants has been criticised. In many parts of the public sector, flows in from the private sector are opening up as people move in for a short period and then move out again. Some organisations said it was still possible to come in as an administrator and show potential, but this is much less frequently the case than in the past and the big growth areas in HR require distinctly different skill sets. One of our case-study organisations did not recruit directly, but rather employed temporary staff and moved them to permanent roles if they were seen to be functioning effectively.

In **Centrica**, the HR Leadership Team was keen to see transfers in from the line. This enhanced the status of HR and improved its knowledge of the business. Transferees would fit in to generalist or project roles but, apart from learning and development, not to specialist posts. The view of some interviewees was that having line managers join HR was a good thing. Besides business knowledge, they brought a challenge to the function. On the debit side, they lack awareness of the difficulties of implementation and, naturally, HR know-how.

Conclusions

What emerges is a sense of considerable enthusiasm for HR, coupled with a belief that the function is harder to penetrate than it was in the past. The main career streams into HR of significance appear to be:

- Deliberate, or at least semi-deliberate, professional entry via an appropriate degree – this group is the most frustrated.

- Other professional career streams, often involving mid-career entry to relatively senior positions.

- Administrative and clerical stream, often via call centres or general administrative work.

There was a general view that HR was seen as a more attractive work area than previously, with many more graduates drawn to the function. Several individuals commented that breaking into the profession was difficult and individuals can spend a long time doing mundane work before they touch anything of significance. There was a view that new degree courses specialising in HR would increasingly form a route into the function.

3 | Moving around and moving up

Unpicking a career history is fraught with difficulties because the frequency of HR reorganisations (often very recent in our case-study organisations) can make it hard to follow the thread of a past career. Identifying future career opportunities is an equally frustrating pastime, as it is hard to gauge what roles will be accessible to people, based on their experience and aptitude. There is, therefore, a distinct contrast between perspectives when looking backward and looking forward.

A retrospective

Senior people generally had diverse experience within their own organisations and within others. For HR generalists, there may have been a series of job moves with growing responsibility (ascending the hierarchy), with wider experience of different kinds of organisations (job hopping) or different roles within the same organisation (building a portfolio). These lateral moves could be seen as consolidating expertise and experience and providing positive CV evidence. Some of our senior people felt their ascent up the hierarchy had been through repeated demonstration of effective performance when the organisation was put under pressure.

In one case study, the HR manager for Policy and Strategy made a conscious decision to move into an operational area and hence moved to managing a personnel team providing services to a key client group. He did this for six years, during which time he took the HR unit through two major inspections in which they did well. After a big restructure he applied for, and was appointed to, a job back at the centre. When the current head of HR took over he was asked to go to another operational area and head up the HR team there, which he did for a year, during which time he created an HR plan and oversaw them working through an inspection that went well for them. He was then asked to come back to the centre, which he did.

It sometimes takes time and persistence for these attributes to be recognised and we did hear of one situation where external candidates were taken on over the head of our interviewee. The external appointments subsequently failed and our interviewee was asked to help pick up the pieces.

The head of HR in one organisation created a departmental personnel section in 1991 and she was asked to head it up. For the next seven years she continued to make significant changes in this department, then moved to work in a corporate role. She took a one-year project manager job, centred on improving HR. At this stage, the organisation had a head of HR who was not visionary and who moved on. This was a catalyst for our interviewee to realise that she needed to achieve a CIPD qualification which she did by a competency assessment route.

The head of HR job was put out to external advert and someone was brought in, but left after nine months. It was at this stage that she was asked to act up and take the personnel unit through a major assessment. This review identified the HR service as one of the top quartile performers in the country and, subsequently, she was appointed permanently to the head of HR post. Many senior appointees have, however, successfully come from outside the organisation with rather different backgrounds.

It is increasingly common in the public and voluntary sectors to make senior appointments from the private sector. For instance, the head of HR at Cancer Research UK came from outside the voluntary sector, and the HR director at Guy's and Thomas' NHS trust came from the finance sector.

Career horizons are viewed very differently from different points in the HR hierarchy. During

'In several of our case studies, junior people were often clearer about where their next move would be than were their senior colleagues.'

much of a career, the focus is upwards: considering how to make beneficial moves (within or outside the organisation), how to position one's experience and take advantage of development opportunities. In several of our case studies, junior people were often clearer about where their next move would be than were their senior colleagues. This was partly a result of there being more jobs available at more junior levels and partly because career options seemed clearer to more junior staff.

There are different issues for specialists. For some specialists there can be quite a limited career horizon, for example, in one of our case-study organisations, one individual in a Health and Safety role commented that there was no further progression possible within this specialism. In this same organisation, several individuals at middle ranking, specialist posts did not intend to stay in that particular specialism, but contemplated a move back to being a generalist or to a different specialist post.

The impact of these various factors is that career options can tighten as individuals ascend a career hierarchy and it becomes more difficult to see where the next move might be. Once a certain level is reached, however, it is as if people emerge from an aspirational funnel and find that there are opportunities all around them. At this point, career options open out and individuals can contemplate senior HR positions or consultancy roles, as well as considering moves to different sectors or kinds of organisations. For example, in our local authority case study, senior individuals spoke of a range of career options that were open to them, (including moving into academia, although this option was made less attractive because of the poor pay), moving out of HR into other senior positions or contemplating independent consultancy.

Our survey has shown that the more senior the role the more likely it is that people will be headhunted and this also creates a wider horizon at senior levels. The survey suggests that around one-quarter of directors (26 per cent) and 17 per cent of senior executives obtained their current post this way. Across the sample as a whole, headhunting accounts for about five per cent of appointments – external application is the most common method of appointment. Our case studies suggest that senior appointments are often made from outside the organisation, suggesting increased organisational mobility at more senior levels.

Tameside authority finds people tend to stay in the HR function. They commented that, typically, local government directors of HR tend to be 'parachuted-in' and, more widely within the sector, there is frequent headhunting of strategic HR people who are considered a scarce resource. There is a skill need for strategic thinking and political ability, as the political dynamic can be very difficult. All those looking back who were now in consultancy, agreed that 'real world' or practical experience before moving to consultancy was essential. This could be acquired successfully in either line management or HR – both had their advantages.

Specialist/generalist choices

There are also those whose aspirations were never upwards and who firmly see a portfolio career for themselves within their existing organisation, specifically those in generalist roles. The distinction between a generalist and a specialist career path can be blurred for some, and many generalists deliberately set out to undertake a range of more specialist roles before moving on or returning to a generalist position. The rationale here is to develop the broad lateral experience we mentioned earlier. For many of those currently in HR specialisms, this is the norm in development terms, as it is unlikely that the specialism will support much hierarchical career movement. There are, however, some specialisms – reward (especially in larger organisations), development/OD, employee relations and, to a lesser extent, resourcing – where the specialism is in sufficient demand to create a career focus. Experience of some of these may be critical for a senior specialist post and absence of a degree of specialist experience at some stage in a career could leave individuals feeling they had a gap in skills which might be career-limiting at senior levels.

In the **Prudential**, generalists build up skills by taking quite specialised posts in both early- and mid-career in a range of areas of HR. These are interspersed with more obviously generalist roles in local units or (now) in service centres or business partner roles. There was general agreement among interviewees that a sensible HR career path often means moving between generalist roles and more specialised areas of work.

The area most obviously seen as sustaining a more specialist career in its own right was learning and development, especially as it now overlaps with both assessment work and OD. Senior people who had little experience of learning and development felt they had some gaps in their skills as a result, especially in coaching.

By contrast, some other areas, such as reward, were seen as possible career areas for those seeking to work as consultants, but the view was expressed that, within organisations reward was more easily seen as part of wider career in HR. Career paths in internal HR functions also depend on how the market for advisory expertise operates. Reward is an example of an area where external advice is often useful and easily available, reducing the need for internal HR people to be quite so specialist.

In **Centrica**, those with a generalist background could move in and out of roles more easily in some situations. It was easier to go to more junior jobs and into certain disciplines, like learning and development. Indeed, it was suggested that to aspire to an HR director job, you had to have rounded experience in both HR and learning and development. Other work areas, like reward, tended to need expertise from the outset. This made it more likely that appointments would be made from the outside.

For those with largely specialist experience, it was more difficult to move into a generalist job without having to move down before moving up. It was said that if one stayed a specialist then there was a real risk of being 'pigeon-holed'.

Within **Guy's and St Thomas'** trust, the specialists had quite varied views as to their next career move. One thought that the next step might be to move back into more generalist HR through a sideways move. Upward progression was believed to be less likely, as there were fewer opportunities at higher levels and roles tended to be occupied by people who were still mid-career and who might not move on. It was also the case that not all wanted the inevitable stress that comes with a more senior role; in fact, some were unsure where they could go next. The possibilities for internal progression were felt to be easier at more junior levels.

Another specialist thought the next logical step would be to take up another specialism and that there was merit in ticking off a number of specialist roles. For them, being a deputy director or director would be perhaps the next big step after another couple of years.

In our outsourced case study, it was felt that movement became more difficult with increasing specialism. It was felt that the outsourcing model was an inhibiter to career opportunities and development, as the client cannot be expected to

> **'For specialists, a career might be seen as *across* organisations rather than *within* an organisation, and this leads to a different outlook on the HR role.'**

bear the cost of developing staff into more specialised roles. For specialists, a career might be seen as *across* organisations rather than *within* an organisation, and this leads to a different outlook on the HR role. Generalists are likely to become quite organisationally-focused, seeing their main loyalty as towards the effective and efficient running of the organisation. Specialists may feel their main loyalty being to their professional expertise, as indeed, earlier research has suggested. We heard support for this view in one of our case studies, when an interviewee said that part of the decision process in determining whether to move to a specialist or generalist position is a political one. HR director posts were seen as committed to corporate goals, whereas specialist roles could be more about professional values and supporting the employee as well as the employer. The career choice to go for an HR director post is, therefore, about orientation as well as ability.

Naturally, the choice of direction – specialist or generalist – depends on personal preferences. Those individuals who prefer strategic interventions and close working with line colleagues, like the business partner posts. Those who enjoy more hands-on, operational activities are likely to opt for service delivery roles. By contrast, those who prefer depth of expertise may opt for specialist posts. By and large, we found that most people were round pegs in round holes; only one or two respondents were frustrated by being miscast.

Our survey shows that generalists and specialists have different views on the value of their career choice. Predictably, generalists are less likely than average to agree that 'Specialists in HR have better career prospects' and more likely to agree that 'Generalists have better prospects in HR'. More surprisingly, they are less likely to agree that

'Experience in another function furthers HR careers'. Specialists, apart from being more likely to agree that that 'Specialists in HR have better career prospects', also tend to favour large organisations. They are more likely to agree that 'To progress in HR, you need to work for a large organisation' and less likely to agree that 'Small and medium organisations offer valuable HR experience'. They are more pessimistic than generalists about their own organisation's requirement for HR practitioners in the future, and about the prestige of HR as a profession.

Horses for courses

HR is not homogenous and the reality is that different kinds of HR careers have different attributes that act to pull quite different kinds of people into the function. A career as an HR consultant, for example, is seen to offer the chance to have an effect relatively quickly which other roles may not. It can seem a much more attractive option than being a relatively junior person in an internal HR team with little chance to make a strategic impact. In this situation, it may often feel like a very slow climb to any role where the opportunity exists to make a real difference to the business. Consultancy also provides the chance to develop some key business skills, such as selling, and appeals to those who 'enjoy the chase,' as much as the 'kill'. It also suits those who like the uncertainty of an unpredictable career. For consultants, and for those working for a service supplier, there is the advantage of being on the revenue not cost side of the business. It gives commercial experience and challenge.

For those in mainstream HR, the points made in Chapter 2 apply. Internal HR work gives exposure to the whole business and the chance to influence it. Whether someone chooses internal HR or management consultancy 'depends on where one

> **'In some organisations, difficult and demanding clientele may make it risky to expose more junior people to responsibility until they have acquired the credibility to hold their own.'**

gets one's kicks'. The former is strong on the content of the work; the latter is more people-focused. Business partners may see their career in terms of a number of job moves but not necessarily to the top, with some commenting that the character of the job becomes quite different at that stage and much more political.

In **Cancer Research UK**, one experienced professional identified a key career decision point as whether to work towards a director-level post in HR by 'climbing the greasy pole', or to work more as an expert, perhaps by moving into self-employment.

In **Centrica**, none of the interviewees admitted to wanting to be the group HR director. Several explicitly said that they would not want the lifestyle or the politics of such a job.

Hopes for the future

There are some early and key career moves that seem to be very difficult because they require a step change in levels of responsibility and autonomy. Most entry-level jobs are highly operational, with clear guidelines and often quite limited task focus. Typically, HR assistant roles are seen as some distance from HR adviser roles, the first real professional level. Making the jump was regarded as quite daunting, and positioning oneself so as to gain appropriate opportunities hard to manage (often a reason for people taking a CIPD qualification at this point). In some organisations, difficult and demanding clientele may make it risky to expose more junior people to responsibility until they have acquired the credibility to hold their own. This, unfortunately, can mean a long haul in career terms and relatively limited early opportunities for individuals to 'cut their teeth'.

In the current structure in **Cancer Research UK**, there are possible moves from the entry-level jobs as HR assistant in the Service Centre and in areas such as resourcing, into HR adviser roles in one of the more specialist teams, or as generalist HR advisers looking after part of the organisation. In practice, the move from assistant to adviser is quite a big job jump – the real move into a professional role.

In a relatively small team, such as within **Lovells**, it can sometimes be more difficult to generate opportunities for upward movement, as the number of senior HR roles is inevitably limited. This presents a challenge in developing the 'next generation' of talent who are keen to progress. Lovells has managed this by encouraging individuals to take on increased responsibility within their existing roles and then recognising these new responsibilities with a promotion to assistant HR manager or HR officer, as appropriate. Another solution has been to offer individuals a chance to 'cut their teeth' on more complex tasks, by supporting them with on-the-job coaching, or allowing them to shadow more experienced managers.

Other transitions are also becoming more difficult with the growth of new models of HR. Most junior people anticipated moving out of their current organisation within the medium term. This may be because attitudes to careers have shifted, or because the restructuring of HR means that they had not been in a role for very long and felt quite fluid in career terms. Another option is that people can struggle to see how they might develop internally, precisely because of the role-segmentation described above. Only those junior staff who could see, or were on, a clear career trajectory within their current organisation were considering staying.

These points only apply to those who saw that they had a career at all – if we define a career as 'onward and upward'. For example, in one organisation, all those we interviewed anticipated staying on in the same organisation. They were predominantly administrators by background and it may be that their entry route limited their career ambitions. Lifestyle may also be a factor here with the advantages proffered by local jobs in less buoyant labour markets also resulting in a different perspective.

Our case studies suggest that there is a key difference between those who quite deliberately contemplate and plan their career and those who take a more relaxed approach. Planning a career seems to be increasingly essential for those who are ambitious and was the norm for younger individuals who saw themselves as HR specialists. Their career-planning horizon tended towards one role, or two to three years ahead. It was striking that many younger interviewees were quite deliberative regarding their career prospects. This contrasted with older interviewees, whose careers were a mix of some key decisions, but with generally little sense of deliberate planning.

Ticket to travel

The CIPD qualification is seen as an essential 'ticket to travel', without which moves within and between organisations become much more difficult. However, interviewees were much stronger in their opinions of it as a market signal (or 'badge') than in the qualification necessarily providing key competencies that were required for professional functioning. Organisations see the CIPD qualification as assisting their endeavours to raise the professional standing of their HR function and as a quality check. Individuals see it as almost essential to be considered for professional HR roles (although clear evidence of expertise and ability might suffice in some sectors).

There are, however, much more mixed views as to its value in the function itself. Some thought it definitely helped people take a much broader and integrated perspective. They felt there was a real step difference in calibre between those who possessed the qualification and those who did not. Others, however, were less positive, and did not see any clear difference in ability between the qualified and unqualified. They saw the qualification as vital to get *in*, but not to get *on*.

One specific angle in this debate is how to treat those entering HR from the line, in mid career. Nobody suggested that HR directors from outside HR should be required to sit CIPD exams but, at least in one organisation, there had been a lively debate about whether business partners should be CIPD-qualified. The company decided that such a requirement would block line managers from applying – a situation it wished to avoid. This decision was not universally welcomed because some HR staff felt that it downgraded the importance of professionalism that, in other respects, the company supported.

Our survey respondents also commented on the factors they thought were important in promoting an HR career. Respondents were asked about a range of factors that might be important to them when pursuing an HR career – in the past, now, or in the future. Figure 5 (opposite) shows a fair degree of clarity about what was important in the past compared to now, with some things (for example, academic qualifications) lessening in importance, while many others (such as business awareness and strategic thinking) being far more important. The future appears to be much less clear in people's minds, however. Just eight of these aspects were seen as having a definite trajectory; academic and vocational qualifications were seen as having less importance over time,

Figure 5 | Important factors when pursuing an HR career

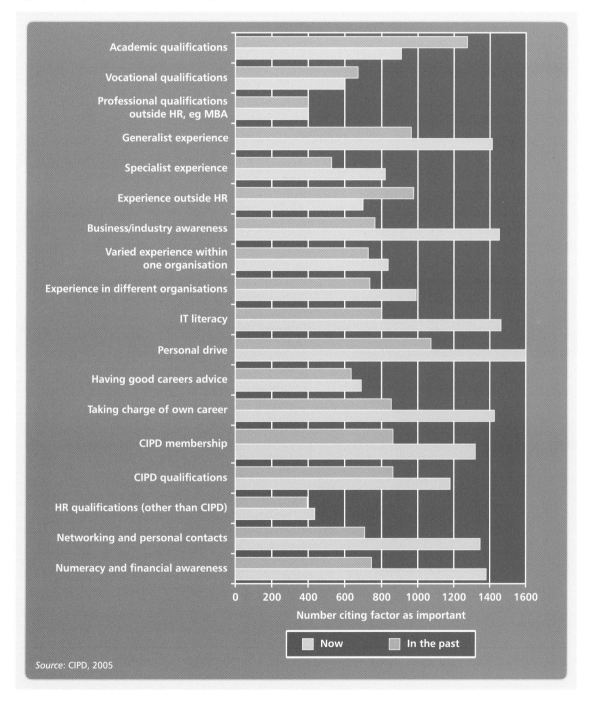

Source: CIPD, 2005

while specialist experience, both outside HR and in different organisations, HR qualifications apart from CIPD, strategic thinking and consultancy skills were all seen as consistently increasing in importance.

When asked which had been the three most important contributors to respondents' HR careers to date, two aspects (personal drive and generalist experience) came out clearly as the top two.

Impact of new structures of HR

The new structures of HR described in Chapter 1, had been adopted in most of our case studies but not all, and were still establishing themselves within organisations. Their impact on career opportunities and transitions were, however, already of concern, especially where reorganisations are becoming ever more frequent. In particular, segmenting the structure into discrete units has led to segmenting the HR population with transitions between groups far from straightforward. In many organisations, there were fears that this would inhibit career entry to certain groups and disrupt existing career pathways, in the absence of alternatives having evolved. Some of the issues raised were:

◘ The disruption of traditional routes from the administrative function into 'professional' roles.

◘ The difficulty of finding suitable recruits for business partner roles.

◘ Huge skill gaps for existing HR administrators to close before being able to make the move to business partner.

◘ Those in shared service functions becoming isolated (physically, organisationally and

content-wise) from other HR jobs, restricting further career progression.

◘ Shared service centres becoming distant from the rest of the organisation and, therefore, finding good relationships difficult to build and maintain.

◘ Similarly, outsourced providers finding it more difficult to formulate effective working relationships within the organisation.

The newer roles of business partner can seem attractive, promising interaction with the business, taking a whole system perspective and building deep relationships with line partners. How people enter business partner roles seemed to still be evolving in organisations. For some, the move tends to be from OD or learning and development roles – because of their existing experience of acting as an internal consultant. In another organisation, movement was facilitated from the shared service centre to more specialist advice roles, which might provide a progression route to business partner. For many organisations, the flow into business partner roles was problematic and both organisations and individuals commented on how difficult this already was. A key question is the balance between internal transfer and external recruitment to the business partner roles. The organisation may look outside to staff these critical jobs, but they risk sending a signal to internal candidates that they are not capable of being developed into these positions.

In **Centrica**, some interviewees felt that getting into HR and moving around within it had become more difficult in the new structure. Previous entry routes (like the HR co-ordinator, a junior field position) had disappeared with the centralisation of administration. And, for

> 'The general reputation of an organisation seemed to be an important factor in contemplating career moves...'

reasons of geography, those who did not live near the Staines shared services centre, were not able to take advantage of the jobs there. If one was not careful, there would be 'big steps' out of shared service jobs (where it was hard to acquire professional qualifications) and from delivery to business partner roles (if knowledge of the more strategic business issues was not developed in the delivery jobs).

In **Hays**, as the current structure is newly in place, it is hard to be definite about career routes. These have shifted (and will shift again) as the HR organisation evolves. The physical separation of the shared service centre means there is no movement between it and the rest of the function. There is limited scope for transfers to and from the consultancy team, given its size. Short-term assignments to work on specific projects are possible, but there has to be back-filling to cover staff absence. There is less flexibility than in a conventional HR team because, in this outsourcing model, charge-out regimes need to be considered. In addition, the client cannot be expected to suffer depleted resources to facilitate support to a change project, even if it is for business reasons.

In the **Prudential** model, the more specialised roles in the service centres do work with managers out in the business, so it is not a 'back-room' role. This business exposure is also seen as an important development for people working in specialist roles and enables them to move later into business partner or senior leadership roles in HR.

This does enable career progression, for example, from the Ask HR helpdesk to an employee relations adviser in the Service Centre, and then on to an employee relations consultant. Likewise, people from the shared service operation can move into junior trainer roles, although reaching the more senior role of development consultant requires more specialist know-how. Once someone has progressed through a range of more specialist roles, they

might be able to move into a junior business partner role. A senior business partner would be likely to have managed an SPC.

Finding a good career path out of the business partner role is something of a challenge, partly because such roles are fairly new in the HR labour market. A business partner could move on to be an HR director in a small organisation, or a specialist in employee relations or change management.

Playing the game

There are many considerations influencing the career moves HR professionals have made or seek to make. Considerations of the kind of organisation, the opportunities it can offer and the dangers attached to making a switch may all influence career choices.

The general reputation of an organisation seemed to be an important factor in contemplating career moves, as there are organisations that were seen to offer very positive CV-building opportunities. Larger household names were regarded positively, especially for more senior roles, and the chance of international work can prove especially compelling. In addition, there was believed to be easier movement between certain sectors than others, eg retail and finance were believed to have affinities.

In **Cancer Research UK**, interviewees commented that the general reputation of the organisation is an important factor when considering a career move in HR – getting 'big name' organisations on one's CV can be an advantage when going for more senior roles. Experience of working for an international company is also seen as a useful CV enhancer and as interesting learning.

HR people in **Prudential** do see sectoral labour markets within HR, both within financial services and also between this sector and others with a consumer sales and service emphasis.

You can move fairly easily between related sectors – such as retail and financial services – but I would find it difficult in manufacturing or science-based sectors. I would also find the public sector difficult and would miss the commerciality.

By contrast, there seemed to be a number of career-limiting situations. Staying too long in one place can have that effect, and several interviewees mentioned that it was important not be seen to become too institutionalised. For example, some in professional consultancy roles suggested that HR experience was important but could be overdone. It was difficult to move into a consultancy firm once you had past a certain level of seniority.

The fear of becoming stuck, in career terms, was greater in certain sectors. For example, the legal world was seen to operate a particularly insular labour market, especially at senior levels. Public sector employees were perhaps the most nervous of their career experiences being viewed negatively. Some felt the experiences they gained were undervalued in the marketplace, despite the fact that significant dealings with some of the more difficult aspects of HR, such as grievances, disciplinaries and tribunal hearings were all much more common in the public sector.

We had comments in the **Home Office**, alluding to the need to think carefully about whether (and when) to move out of the organisation because of what might be conceived as a 'public-sector stigma'. Staying for two to three years was seen to be ok, but staying for longer might reduce future job market opportunities.

Other *cul de sacs* seemed to arise from role rather than choice of organisation or sector. Back-office functions may be disconnected from the rest of the organisation and career paths may feel very truncated.

Perhaps because of their unique situation, outsourced providers may offer relatively limited scope for experience. This may occur due to tight resourcing approaches within the client organisation, or because there is not a tradition (or simply not the opportunities) to move within the contractor firm.

Major career moves between organisations can be seen to be a combination of positive and deliberate career strategy, ie looking for an appropriate move and taking the opportunity when it occurs, or precipitated by reorganisations or job losses. Several interviewees had been made redundant from previous posts and had, therefore, experienced a 'career push', as opposed to a career jump. HR professionals were also more likely to leave an organisation where the climate was one of sustained cost-cutting: perhaps preferring to jump rather than be pushed, but more likely to mention the lack of job satisfaction.

It was noted in one of our case studies that career moves between organisations were quite often precipitated by reorganisations or the threat of possible job loss. Working in organisations suffering prolonged periods of cost-cutting also took much of the satisfaction out of HR work and had caused people to move on.

In the **Prudential,** interviewees commented that career moves between organisations had often been precipitated by reaching the top of a particular career ladder and 'feeling stuck' or running out of career options within an organisation unless willing to consider a geographical move. Some people in that situation will prefer to move company rather than go for a more senior job involving a major relocation.

Conclusions

It is clear that mapping out a career in HR is not straightforward and there are many considerations for those who want to see their career progress. For many people, there is a need to consider the implications of three possible career moves: sector; organisation; role.

The public sector can provide considerable experience in areas that are less common elsewhere, eg disciplinaries, grievances and tribunal hearings. The public sector would appear to be (from our case studies) more willing to develop people into HR and to help them achieve a qualification and, in larger organisations, or where there is a strong sectoral identity, can provide considerable career opportunities. However, too long in the public sector may affect the ease with which HR practitioners can move into the private sector.

The organisation is important because of the range of experience it can provide and the way it structures HR. Certain 'big names' appear to be CV-enhancing as does working for a global organisation. Small organisations can, however, provide a breadth of experience that would be difficult to find elsewhere.

Finally, many of the concerns we heard expressed focused on job role. The tension between generalist and specialist roles and finding the right

balance between them is a major concern. The impact of new forms of HR is yet to be fully seen.

Individuals wanting to successfully climb an HR career ladder need to contemplate these options carefully and consider, not just their current job, but look at least one role ahead. Unless a specialist career appeals, it would seem to be advisable to consider a range of specialisms for relatively short periods or to zigzag backwards and forwards between specialist and generalist roles.

Organisations need to be aware of the frustrations of younger entrants in accessing and progressing in an HR career. New structures are in danger of closing off career opportunities and limiting the traditional junior flows into the function. We have seen that some organisations have given this considerable thought and put in place practices that act to encourage movement and grow experience, but others have travelled less far along this path and could benefit from a review of practice.

New structures have created new skill needs and most organisations are struggling to a degree to fill business partner roles. Thinking through how people can develop the relevant career skill sets will, we suspect, be an issue for many organisations.

There has also been a move to increase the professionalisation of the HR function in recent years, which has meant an increased entry of graduates. On the whole, this is seen to be a good thing, but organisations may need to think carefully about how they intend to grow and develop this cadre, so that they do not become stuck and frustrated.

4 | Moving on

What the future holds for HR professionals who seek to move on, is dependent very much on their previous career histories and the opportunities it offers them.

Out of current job in corporate HR

A number of possible career routes out of an individual's current job within corporate HR were seen as possible. These included into line management, a move to consultancy, to another organisation or to a completely different career.

Into line management

This choice was felt to be severely constrained by the core work of the organisation and the degree of specialisation involved. Where generalist managers existed, the possibility of transferring into a more corporate role could be seen as possible, but where non-HR roles in the organisation are very specialist in nature, requiring professional skills and knowledge, any such transfer is impossible.

In the **Centrica** HR team, a move into line management was seen to be one of several possible moves, but was considered to be difficult. The general view was that, even if there have been successes in the past, this would be difficult to achieve, particularly for those who had already achieved middle-management status. It would be hard to secure a lateral move. Business experience was likely to be better achieved through working in a multidisciplinary team on a project with a strong people component. This can be high-profile and business-critical.

In **Hewitts**, a switch to corporate life, but not in an HR role, seemed to be of somewhat more interest. However, the interviewees suggested certain conditions would have to be met. They would need to feel they had an affinity with, and preferably knowledge of, the sector. The

organisation itself would ideally be in a phase of change, where consultancy skills could be deployed. It was thought that organisations committed to the status quo would not be suitable for most consultants.

HR business partners who have left the HR in the **Prudential** have gone into quite varied types of work, including line management within the company and managing an outsourced HR supplier.

A move to consultancy

Consultancy was an option for some because of the attraction of work in a more specialist field and the greater variety. However, this was often seen as a late career move. Others were less positive, believing that the big HR consultancy firms had lost some of their appeal because they were thought to work people too hard, and independent consultancy was seen as too 'scary' due to the high levels of business failure after a year or two. The view that 'you do not see the end product of your efforts' in consultancy was also frequently expressed.

In **Centrica**, consultancy was one of the possible career routes out of the Centrica HR team, although there was the risk that one would miss the benefit of seeing tasks through to a conclusion, but with the benefit of lots of varied project work. Some participants felt that large consultancies did not have the kudos they had in the past. They have a reputation for 'bleeding you dry'.

In **Hays** the move to independent consultancy was not seen very positively. Some of the participants had had prior experience of independent consultancy, albeit for relatively short periods. Such a move was seen as a bit 'scary' because you have to be self-reliant and win all

'...the majority of respondents think that it is advisable to move around in an HR career, and get experience in different functions, sectors and organisations, rather than sticking to one.'

your own work. It could be exciting, though, if one was successful. Generally, participants saw consultancy as a future option, for later in one's career when one could offer more experience. Moreover, it was noted that it often took a life-changing event (eg redundancy) to push people into such a move.

Career paths out of internal HR work are potentially different in a firm like **Hewitts**. There are opportunities to move into the company's consultancy practice, as well as self-employment as an independent consultant. The latter option also applies to those working in the consultancy practice. Viewed from an internal HR role, consultancy is seen to have pros and cons. It offers a focus on delivery. It avoids the problem of internal politics. But the downside is that you do not see your contribution all the way through delivery and beyond.

To another organisation

On the whole people were quite thoughtful about what they needed to do next in career terms and would consider opportunities which broadened them either in terms of the kinds of organisation they worked for (size or sector), the role they did (specialist or generalist) or the level of responsibility they had (a move up the ladder). The opportunity for international experience was seen positively by those seeking a predominantly private-sector career. To some, small organisations were desirable early in a career because they could offer greater responsibility.

In **Centrica**, interviewees commented on the possibility of moving to another company, possibly in another sector, to give broader HR experience, or, smaller size, to be more able to demonstrate value or to a role with more international exposure.

Interviewees in the **Hays** HR team believed that the most realistic option for them was to move to another internal HR position in another company. Many staff are wedded to staying in the local area, so there is a limited choice of employers. When asked whether they would choose to work with an outsourced service provider again, mixed views were given. The majority had their doubts. The minority, represented particularly by those who came from Liverpool Victoria were more positive.

For more experienced people in the **Prudential**, if they left the business they might consider moving into a more international HR role – seen as a key experience. Options also include moving to similar roles in other companies, working in outplacement or, for some, moving into line management and staying there.

In **Guy's and Thomas'** Trust, there was a view that most people who moved away from the Trust tended to remain in HR and in the NHS. Some people have moved out of the Trust to the private sector and some have left and come back. There were some examples of people leaving for other parts of the public sector, for example the police, and others to smaller Trusts so they could have jobs with greater responsibility.

The survey found that the majority of respondents think that it is advisable to move around in an HR career, and get experience in different functions, sectors and organisations, rather than sticking to one. They also view small and medium organisations as offering valuable experience, and feel that it is not necessary to work in a large organisation to progress. Exposure to both the public and private sectors is viewed favourably, while almost half also feel that international experience improves HR career prospects, too. Generalists are perceived as having better career prospects than specialists.

To a completely different career

We have already quoted academia as a possible career change. Other considered career changes can be many and varied. There was some sense in which this was a case of the 'grass is greener' elsewhere, but either for those early in their career (where HR may not have proved to be what they wanted) or late in the career (to do something different before retirement) this could be a positive choice.

> One interviewee contemplated moving away from HR into employment as a psychotherapist, as this was an area in which he had a qualification.

> Another was on the point of leaving his company to become a maths teacher.

There are sectoral differences in this overall picture. Local government, for example, is more self-contained in career terms than others. It would tend to grow its own, and senior people tend to see their career in terms of local government rather than a single authority. HR for legal firms is, as we have said, quite insular. HR consultancy organisations offer their internal HR community the potential for rather different career paths. There are opportunities to move from an internal HR provider into the consultancy practice, and in this environment individuals are less negative about such a shift. This seems to be easier at more junior levels or where there is similarity in the type of work (from internal to external consultancy). The move to consultancy has both advantages and disadvantages, such roles are much more clearly focused on delivery with rapid interventions and withdrawal. They can also avoid the worst of internal organisational politics but these advantages are also the downside, failing to allow

the opportunity for real in-depth engagement with an organisation and its people.

Or, staying put...

A difficulty for those who want to move on is deciding at what point to do so. There is clearly a tension for those trying to build a portfolio, about staying in one place for too long, and yet, if the current organisation is a good one and seems to offer good opportunities, there is an equal desire to stay. There are also those who anticipate staying for some time. Stayers do so either because of a sense of loyalty and commitment to the organisation, or because it suits them in some more transactional way, eg it is near to home, or because they have looked elsewhere, but have not been able to find anything better. In this sense, HR may not be that different from many other careers.

> In **Centrica**, staff generally seemed keen to stay and those that faced career blockages were either resigned to limited movement or hoped that further organisational change would bring new opportunities. Those who took this view did so out of 'loyalty' to the company or because it was 'difficult to find a better job'. For people who thought more seriously about life outside Centrica, staying with the firm gave lots of useful experience. Judging when to leave would always be difficult and affected by personal circumstances, but the drivers would still be there: not to remain at the same company for '30 years', to gain wider professional exposure and to fulfil personal ambitions.

> In **Cancer Research UK**, some of the younger staff interviewed felt rather 'stuck' in junior roles and could not see how they would progress. However, they also found employment agencies were not good at suggesting other kinds of work they might look at. Some felt they had taken so long to get a foothold in HR that it was better to 'hang in there' and hope for opportunities to progress.

In the **Home Office**, there was very little expressed desire to move out of HR. Most individuals saw themselves as remaining in the function and many thought the Home Office offered such good career opportunities, they would choose to stay in the organisation. For the few who did contemplate a move away from HR, they spoke about a move into a more general management role, with one commenting that this would be good for understanding engagement. Despite the growing professionalisation of HR in the civil service, there were still a few who thought they would move on into other civil service roles and, therefore, saw their stay in HR firmly in terms of a wider civil service career.

Moving on from consultancy

By contrast, those we spoke to who were already occupying a consultancy role were much less keen to move direction to a role in the HR function. The loss of a range of clients and the variety and strategic nature of the work is seen as a major disincentive. Life in corporate HR was also seen as more isolating, especially for those in senior roles compared to the teamworking which exists in a consultancy firm, and the support this offers. Consultants also possess a very distinct skill set and are motivated by making a difference within organisations. A move to a management role might be considered if these key skills could still be utilised.

In **Hewitts**, none of our case-study consultants were particularly interested in a move to an HR function. One individual had considered, but rejected the idea. There is a fear that one would lose variety in the work and not have the challenge of dealing with multiple clients. There is, moreover, a fear that life can be very 'lonely' at the top of the HR hierarchy – one can be very 'isolated' and 'exposed'. This is to be contrasted with the teamworking ethos of a good consultancy like Hewitts, where you can share knowledge and build long-term relationships. This can provide benefits in delivering good project results, but also offer emotional support. There is always the realisation that dealing with a difficult client is only a temporary phenomenon. Nonetheless, there is peer support available, if needed.

For a few, self-employment has its appeal, as it avoids some of the negatives of organisational life and holds the promise of being able to structure your life to suit. Compared with being an employed consultant, there is the advantage of receiving the entire fee. However, for those already working in consultancy, there is the danger of losing access to the knowledge of colleagues or being able to pool resources on large projects. You also lose access to the networks of contacts and have to forge your own. So self-employment was generally viewed with some anxiety as potentially risky, something that might be better considered at the end of a career.

In **Hewitts**, self-employment has its appeal because you can avoid the internal politics of working in a large organisation and the management tasks (if these do not appeal). You can structure your life to fit in with your own sense of work–life balance, rather than your employer's. You control what you do, how you do it and for whom. Compared with being an employed consultant, you can 'earn the whole fee!' On the debit side, as against internal HR, you do not always see what you have delivered. In contrast with being part of a firm of consultants, you do not have access to the knowledge or resource pool to help out with difficult or large projects. (Networking with like souls can mitigate against this problem to a degree.) For both groups, you have to like selling and be persistent. The common complaint is that you have 'exhausted your business card list' after 18 months or so.

'**Interviewees, considering moves to other firms, also stressed the importance of the values of the organisation they might join.**'

As we have already remarked, moving to academia is an option for those leaving consultancy (and indeed more senior people in organisations). It has the advantage of giving people an opportunity to reflect on what they know, to study further, and to be able to teach others. But these benefits are not matched by financial rewards and this can be a major disincentive.

In **Hewitts**, academia is, on the face of it, a realistic option for consultants. It gives the chance to study and reflect in depth in areas where you have worked. There is also an attraction to teaching – being able to pass on knowledge and experience, and make a difference to people's lives. In other words, it offers 'self-actualisation.' But there are downsides in terms of the pay and the politics.

Interestingly, those in consultancy did not see the move to a different consultancy firm as a significant opportunity. There seemed to be few gains, the only reason for such a move would be to take advantage of a particular niche opening or because the current employer disappointed in some way. Critical in the choice of firm is whether its 'values' fitted personal principles.

Interviewees, considering moves to other firms, also stressed the importance of the values of the organisation they might join. This seems to be especially important in consulting. Why would you move to another consultancy firm unless either you want to develop a niche work area or your present employer fails to keep their proposition in line with the market? Assuming what is on offer fits with what you want, you are better to continue with an organisation you are already committed to.

Conclusions

Inevitably, the decisions on whether and where to move on to are very individual in nature:

Choice in these matters will always be very personal and depend upon your own circumstances. Issues like financial security, family ties, location, are all important. What challenges you as an individual can be key.

We have seen that, for some individuals and some organisations, the move from HR to line management is seen to be a positive option, as indeed is a move from the line into HR. Where this is possible, there are benefits both ways, and organisations ought to think carefully about how they can help to facilitate these moves. However, the major routes out of the existing role/organisation are to another HR role, often in another organisation. Individuals are motivated by new responsibilities, and the acquisition or broadening of specialist knowledge. For those relatively early in their career, the main concern is to acquire jobs with greater responsibility.

5 | The joys and frustrations of an HR career

The attractions of the function

Our survey gave a very clear message: the vast majority of respondents are very positive about an HR career. When asked, 'If you could start your career again from the beginning, would you still opt for HR?', the large majority (81 per cent) said 'yes'. The reasons given were mostly related to variety, challenge, interest and enjoyment, and the view that HR is at the heart of the business and offers an opportunity to make a difference; many respondents also felt it suited their particular abilities. A selection of representative comments is given in Table 1, on page 38.

Our case studies also found considerable positive regard for the professional standing of the function with nearly all respondents believing that the standing of HR had improved a great deal in their organisations over the past few years. As a result, interviewees mentioned line managers being more willing to seek support from the function.

However, there are undoubtedly also frustrations associated with working in the function and these were recognised, albeit by a minority, in their response to the survey. Those who replied 'no' when asked if they would still opt for HR should they be starting their career again, were less consistent when giving their reasons. Some wished they had opted for a different career altogether, while others were critical of HR's image, positioning and perceived value within the business. Another theme was the hard work and constant, frustrating struggle for recognition.

Being respected

It is not easy, according to some of our case-study participants, to earn the respect of the line and maintain the trust among employees. New models of HR assume that it is an attractive function to work in that has a welcome place in the organisation, and yet in some cases achieving this status can be hard fought. There are still tensions with some managers who regard HR as the source for tea and sympathy, or employees who see the function as a management lackey.

The opinions of managers naturally depended on what sort of experience they had had with HR in the past. But in general, support functions, and HR in particular, are not seen as 'sexy' places to work.

The internal status of HR was not felt to be very high in one case study that had outsourced the function. Management has a rather limited view of what it can achieve, and the decision to outsource was seen to be indicative of this slightly negative view, suggesting that it was seen purely as a service function. It was also felt that the supplier–client distinction can be a barrier. At the individual level, there are mixed experiences. Some managers think that HR staff just 'drink tea and chat' and are a cost on the business. Some think HR is slow, bureaucratic and obstructive. But there are those who value the support they are given.

The relationship of HR to the line was traditionally seen as having been one of dependency. The relationship was characterised as HR used to do everything for managers in the past, whereas now there was a desire to devolve more HR responsibility to the line. This in itself can give rise to adverse views, and it was suggested that some do not want the additional responsibility. Most interviewees felt that HR was not valued highly in the past but that the standing of HR had improved enormously in recent years. Interviewees commented that the growing credibility of the function owed much to its increasing professionalism. Historically, it was felt that the function used to be quite slow in response, whereas the focus now is on providing a solution rather than saying no to line managers. There was felt to be greater awareness of the needs of managers and how to meet them. In response, one interviewee noted that line managers did not now wait for things to go wrong, but came and asked questions.

Table 1 | Why opt for HR?

Comment
'Always changing, varied, interesting career'
'In the right company, you can still make a difference to how people are managed and developed'
'Because of its unpredictability and constant demand for self-development, it drives me mad, but keeps me alive!'
'Brilliant, varied, different every day'
'Developing people and making a real difference to the organisation – getting the organisation to where it needs to be'
'Enjoy being at the heart of the business'
'Excellent opportunity to be involved in all aspects of the business'
'Facilitating organisational and people development is the most rewarding career'
'Fascinating, ever-changing role'
'From a very early career stage you are working at the heart of an organisation'
'Highly-varied, people-oriented and satisfying'
'HR has been a really interesting part of my career'
'I am good at it and it enables involvement in the whole business which other disciplines don't allow'
'I enjoy what I do in a constantly changing company'
'I have enjoyed the career move more than anything else I have ever done'
'I have had 30+ fantastic years and would do it over and over again'
'It's mostly been fun and it fits the way my mind works'
'It best suits my character'
'It took me long enough to find my forte – and I'm good at it!'
'Matches my strengths/talents/values'
'People provide such a variety of challenges – never dull or samey'
'Short-cut to seniority for a female'
'Suits my skill set and I get job satisfaction'
'We can make a difference'

Source: CIPD, 2005.

> **'At present, there appears to be a discord between those who wish to begin a career in HR and the opportunities which are open to them.'**

In professional organisations, there are particular challenges in being accepted as an adviser. To be successful, HR needs to be as skilled and educated as the client, and have the personal skills to be seen as adding value. These include a degree of toughness in being able to handle difficult internal clients. As we have previously commented, this can lead to problems within the function of not wanting to expose people before they are ready.

As a consequence, HR did not always meet the expectations of its newer members, and we heard from individuals the disappointment that sometimes followed from engaging with the reality of the HR world. Desire to make a difference, to be able to engage with a specialism such as employee relations and to make the organisation better-functioning, could wane when confronted with a rigid, rule-bound approach, or by a philosophical mismatch between individual and organisation. This was more likely to happen in early career when a certain idealism met with the reality of work in the function. For our interviewees, this had not resulted in leaving the function, but in making moves within it, eg from personnel to training or from employee relations to OD, to find a stream of work that suited aspirations, interests and values better.

Even some more mature members of the HR community described their difficulties in being accepted. One commented:

90 per cent of clients in one business unit believe they have an excellent service and wouldn't move without our help. The other 10 per cent would spit on us.

Overload

Many operational roles seemed to be very demanding in time and energy. Resources are limited, especially in organisations that see HR as a cost to be contained. Devolvement should have reduced the HR workload, but that presupposes that line managers take on the responsibilities expected of them. Some 'resisted', making life still harder for HR.

Getting on

We have previously commented that HR can feel impenetrable, with the function demanding such high entry criteria that people are either put off or become resentful. At present, there appears to be a discord between those who wish to begin a career in HR and the opportunities which are open to them. Entry-level jobs now demand the CIPD qualification and between two to five years' experience which, for those not even on the ladder, can seem to place it out of reach. Younger entrants commented on having to move around a number of organisations in a range of quite junior roles before being able to find one that would contemplate funding their CIPD course. There were also concerns expressed that the function did not seem to recognise some of the newer forms of qualification that prospective entrants may put forward. HR degrees or degrees where HR is a significant component are becoming increasingly popular, yet do not seem to have found a sufficient market advantage within the HR community. These issues were raised by junior people in some organisations over and over again.

Younger people can also feel rather stuck in junior roles and struggle to see how they might progress. It is difficult to see a route out of HR into something different, and some feel trapped within the function despite the effort they have put in to date.

For those working in commercial settings, there is the added difficulty that staff development has to be paid for. The client is unlikely to be willing and the employer will have to be mindful of getting a return on the investment. Moreover, service levels cannot be allowed to deteriorate while someone is developing into a new role.

In the next chapter, we will turn to what organisations can do to alleviate some of these issues.

6 | Career development and support for learning

In this chapter we look at how individuals are supported in developing their careers in HR, through organisational processes for career development and learning. In both career development and in learning we see differing views and practices in terms of two key dimensions:

◘ The extent to which the employing organisation offers positive support, or whether it is very much left up to individuals to manage their own careers and learning.

◘ The extent to which career and skill development is facilitated by formal processes versus more informal and individualised approaches.

Extent and nature of career development support

Our survey asked respondents about sources of career advice that had been useful to date. The six most frequently cited were, in order from the top: HR press, line manager, CIPD member services, the Internet, friends and relatives, and non-CIPD HR networks. The picture changes somewhat, however, when respondents name the sources that have been the *most influential*: the top six now becomes line manager (a long way ahead of the rest), HR press, friends and relatives, CIPD member services, mentor, and non-CIPD HR networks (see Figure 6, on page 42).

Our case studies provide much more detail. Most of the case organisations had some scope for individuals to develop a career in HR inside the organisation, having a range of work at different levels. But, of course, offering career development in very small organisations is a much greater challenge.

However, there were differences between organisations in the extent to which they were attempting to offer individuals positive support in making career moves and getting the right range of experiences. Most large organisations operate open internal job markets where vacancies are advertised to staff, and the case studies in this research also had this approach. So, in some sense, individuals can progress their careers by applying for vacant jobs. However, some participants commented that their organisations were very risk-averse in making HR appointments and this made it difficult for them to get access to the right range of experiences without some more positive help.

Often, career opportunities were there, but the process of managing a career was informal and *'required the individual to make most of the running'*. Such informal systems predominated in the case organisations, and could be quite effective where the culture was one of offering personal support. Their effectiveness relies on individuals within the function having access to more senior people in HR, who can advise them and do a bit of brokering on their behalf. In this informal model, individuals can be encouraged by a manager or informal mentor to go for a particular post. In other organisations, informal approaches really meant *'sink or swim'* from the perspective of junior staff, and this was not seen as an effective strategy for the future resourcing of the HR function.

In a slightly more formal approach, some of the case organisations used internal secondments (eg Cancer Research UK) or job rotation (eg Prudential) to help broaden individuals' experiences. Several of the organisations had a philosophy among senior HR people of offering more systematic support for career development within HR, but this was not yet very visible to junior staff.

Figure 6 | Most influential sources of career advice

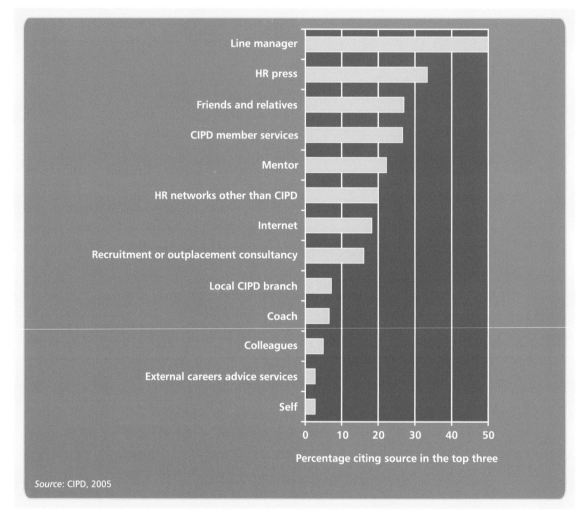

Percentage citing source in the top three

Source: CIPD, 2005

A few cases were seeking to use rather more formal and strategic approaches to career development within HR. For example, the Prudential and Centrica were both trying to take a periodic review of the function and look at the development needed by individuals. This is a form of functional succession and development review. The aim here is often to strengthen learning but also to facilitate moves to give people the broader experience they so often need to move further in their careers.

In **Centrica**, there is 'active' career management from the perspective of the HR leadership team. Regular management meetings are held to look at the performance and potential of the HR population. They aim to move people about to give them a 'broader perspective', and this succeeds across the function because of a growing sense of having a shared resource. This would bring benefits in career opportunities with the size of the organisation that would be missing in a small firm.

> **'...one would say that the clear majority of the case studies *intended* to have more systematic support for HR careers, but had not yet implemented this.'**

A project is being undertaken on career paths. The aim is not to produce something mechanistic, but to aid discussion between the employer and employee. Career planning workshops are being tested and a set of technical and behavioural competencies are being developed. Thought is being given to a set of job families within HR – say generalist, learning and development, reward, resourcing and administrative.

There is also quite conscious career management for HR people in the **Prudential**. This is geared at facilitating moves between generalist early roles and the more specialist work, and at bringing people with expertise into business partner roles. There is also proactive movement of people around business partner roles so they do not stay too long in one part of the business.

The HR management team reviews the careers of staff in the function twice a year and managed moves quite often result as a means of developing potential within the function.

Cancer Research UK had carried out a systematic review of its HR people (using a development centre) a while ago, resulting in some useful career moves internally. But this kind of process had not been repeated recently.

Systematic career development support does require continuous attention if it is to remain effective. Inevitably any process which provides more managed career moves, runs into the problem of feeling unfair to some people. Sometimes, more managed careers will only apply to high fliers or more senior HR people, with more informal processes for the rest.

Processes for giving career advice to HR professionals tend, on the whole, to be fairly haphazard. Some participants were quite wary of having real career discussions with staff in HR. This is quite telling when one considers that the HR function is expecting managers in other functions to do this for their staff. The assumption that career advice can be 'dangerous' also shows misunderstanding about what such discussions should be like, or the problems for both the individual and, indeed, the organisation, of the 'sink or swim' alternative.

Career and learning support during change

As we have seen, the HR function is in a state of flux, with new roles emerging and new career paths having to grow. This change is having a number of impacts on career and skill development for HR people.

Some of the case organisations had used quite systematic approaches to career development in the past, or at least had clear career paths – but these had lapsed during restructuring processes. This resulted in some organisations feeling that they had gone backwards in career-development terms, with diminishing understanding of career paths and how individuals should prepare themselves for job moves. Restructures, and the move to completely new ways of delivering HR were felt to have disrupted traditional patterns. In other organisations, there was a sense that the organisation was seeking to provide more structure and, therefore, understanding of what a career might be. Some of these, such as Centrica, were moving towards a more clearly articulated view of how development should be managed in the HR function. If one had to generalise, one would say that the clear majority of the case studies *intended* to have more systematic support for HR careers, but had not yet implemented this.

As with career development generally, some organisations are choosing to focus first on senior or high-potential staff in HR (the talent management approach), leading to a more segmented policy for career development. One organisation studied was using a matrix to identify performance and potential and, therefore, focus organisational attention and development opportunities on those most likely to succeed.

Seniority can, however, cut both ways. It might be expected that signalling and the grooming of people for more senior roles becomes more explicit in more senior positions but this does not necessarily seem to be the case. In some organisations, the focus of individual discussions shifts from career, to meeting objectives as the individual becomes more senior. This is partly in response to a tightening of opportunities which means the possibility of meeting aspirations lessens and nervousness sets in about having discussions about future career.

As HR jobs change, so do the skills and competencies required. Old competency frameworks can look out-of-date and fail to reflect the emergent function. The business partner role often requires urgent attention and the Home Office, for example, was focusing on equipping people for this role.

There is often a slightly hidden agenda about whether existing HR employees are likely to be able to meet the demands of new job roles. The shift from a focus on administration to one on business partner type role is particularly challenging. This may be making some managers in HR wary of talking to long-established HR people about their future careers.

As might be expected, those working in a consultancy role tended to feel that their career was predominantly self-driven and highly dependent on their own personal capabilities. Consultancy firms tended not to have a formal hierarchy of roles to which people applied and/or were appointed, but rather encouraged growth and rewarded growing capability with a gradual extension of role.

Support for learning

Approach to supporting learning

Philosophies about support for learning and career development are often related. Systematic approaches to career development often go hand-in-hand with well-supported and structured personal and professional development. Such organisations provide considerable support for formal professional development and this might encompass higher level learning and support for the professional development of HR staff. On the other hand, a self-managed career philosophy is more likely to sit alongside self-managed learning.

As we have seen above, support for career development is not especially strong at present. Support for learning and development is, however, generally better, especially for junior HR staff. For outsourced HR providers, there are some tensions around staff development needs and ensuring that the contract is fulfilled and clients' needs met. As a result, the horizon is also nearly always focused on the short to medium term, ie the period until contract renewal, rather than considering development in the longer term. For any investment to be worthwhile, it has to produce benefits in the contract term, unless the benefit is to the supplier company. Whether this is likely to transpire, depends on the resourcing model. If staff are not transferred between contracts, there is much less incentive to encourage learning beyond the specific contract requirements.

Formal training

Most of those interviewed in the case organisations did receive formal training, but not always in a very systematic way. Programmes to support common HR roles, at least at junior levels, may be very helpful in ensuring a baseline of competence. For example, Tameside had very structured training for junior staff joining the training and development function. As mentioned above, the Home Office was paying particular attention to business partner development.

Several of the case-study organisations had quite active individualised development, but little systematic learning based on common role types (eg Centrica, Hays, Hewitts). Line managers often spoke of providing development opportunities for their own more junior staff. These were quite imaginative mixes of workshops, secondments, events and masterclasses.

Formal internal training in the bigger organisations seems to centre on generic skills, especially management-related ones. These courses are available to all HR staff.

Senior people are more likely to see their formal learning as being facilitated by conferences and external events. There were some examples of course attendance, but this was rarer. The one area where some form of external training was becoming more common was in providing development to HR business partners to help them understand the skill needs of this new role.

Consistent with the approach to career management, professional training and development is largely a bottom-up exercise, driven and managed by the individual, especially where it relates to adding skills for future use. Where current job-related skills are required (and this can be the case with a shift to business partners) there tends to be more management insistence, and the provision of collective training. On the whole, training plans are more likely to be individual than role-centred. This model can be a very good one for HR, as long as good development discussions take place to identify individual needs and that these needs are really followed through.

Supporting CIPD study

Certainly several organisations were keen to support the study for CIPD qualifications and/or Masters degrees (in HR or related disciplines). CIPD training is clearly seen as providing the most coherent structure for initial professional knowledge. There are more question marks over whether current CIPD training provides people with the practical skills they need (for example, in talking to managers and employees), as well as their formal knowledge.

The case organisations were quite varied in whether they actually funded CIPD study. Such funding was highly valued by the individuals who received it and perhaps the most important part of the 'development deal', as far as they were concerned. The decision about support for CIPD study could depend on position or role in the organisation as well as which organisation you worked for. The public sector organisations in this study were likely to fund study, often having positive policies in this regard in all professions. Study was also seen as an integral part of raising the professionalism of the function. Cancer Research UK and the Prudential also strongly supported professional study.

> 'Informal learning, close to the job and provided by colleagues, is just as important as more formal learning.'

Informal learning

Informal learning, close to the job and provided by colleagues, is just as important as more formal learning. The focus group discussions highlighted many good examples of buddying, coaching and mentoring.

In Cancer Research UK, for example, a buddying system is used to link people working in the service centre with HR advisers in the business. This gives junior staff a chance to meet managers and employees face-to-face (not just on the phone) and also to get more in-depth experience of problem-solving. Furthermore, it has the business benefit of giving the advisers some more flexible resources. Internal sessions are also provided in the case-study organisations on topics of current importance. Often these are delivered by experienced insiders, or sometimes by external consultants. OD is a hot topic for such sessions. These internal workshops were generally well-received and appreciated by those who had worked in HR for some time, as well as those at earlier stages in their career.

One interesting feature of learning on the job is that it relies on informal relationships forming with colleagues whom you see during the working day. Some of the newer patterns of working may be making this more difficult. For example, shared services may be physically removed from HR experts, and business partners may be located with the line. As a result, communities of practice and the informal transfer of knowledge may not occur naturally and may need positive facilitation. As a result of this situation, the Home Office is seeking to strengthen both internal and external networking opportunities for its HR staff.

Significant work to be done

Overall, it seems that the case-study organisations are struggling to keep their approaches to career and skill development in line with changes to the HR function. Many individuals working in HR were keen for:

◻ a clearer overview of the kinds of roles in HR at different levels, and the kinds of career experiences needed to access such jobs.

◻ more structured career and learning experiences in early career to equip them with an understanding of the function, knowledge of different areas of HR work and the broader skills in business and in influencing to work with the line.

◻ opportunities to move around in HR, compatible with their overall career direction.

◻ more tailored individual learning support, especially as they come into mid-career, where career paths become more varied.

◻ opportunities to engage in internal and external networks.

◻ frank discussion of their career opportunities in the light of their own aptitudes and aspirations.

Organisations that set about offering such support will maintain a good overview of the people in the HR function and those who need particular attention in terms of facilitated moves, secondments, project experiences etc. HR directors have a particular responsibility to offer more robust support and to take their own role as head of profession seriously. Most large organisations expect career development to be a 'partnership' between the organisation and its employees. There is some way to go in making this a reality for employees working in HR.

7 | Professionalisation and the future

There was widespread agreement that the HR function had moved in recent years to become more professional. Most of our case-study organisations and our interviewees within them, believed that the standing of HR had increased by leaps and bounds in their organisations. This did not necessarily mean that HR had to have a place on the board, although it frequently had, but it was now generally seen to be credible and effective.

There were also generally very positive views about the standing of HR as a profession, while opinions on how the function is viewed more widely within the organisation are less positive. Respondents in the survey generally feel that HR is growing in prestige, due in part to the current emphasis on human capital, but only one-third believe that others in their organisations see HR as an attractive place to work. Figure 7, below, shows that there is

Figure 7 | The status of HR, by job level

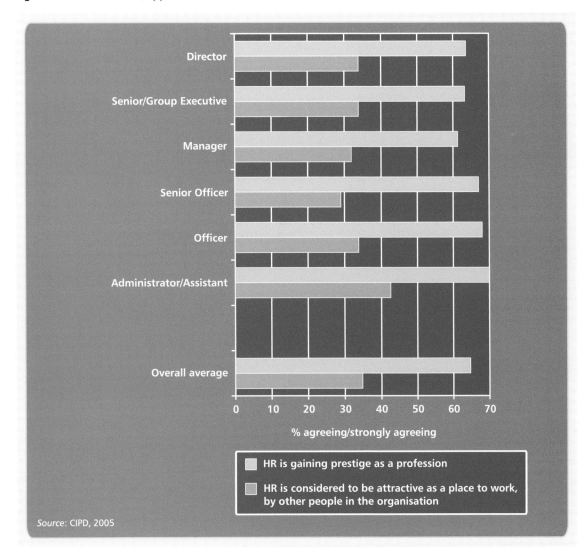

Source: CIPD, 2005

> **'The need for qualified people relates to the ability to credibly deliver the role, to command respect and trust in judgement.'**

some, though not much, variation in views about HR, depending on respondents' level in their organisation. Attitudes towards the following two statements were analysed by job level:

HR is gaining prestige as a profession.

HR is considered to be attractive, as a place to work, by other people in the organisation.

The results show that people occupying relatively junior roles (administrators/assistants) are the most optimistic about HR's status. This may be partly due to the optimism associated with relative 'newness' in the role. Managers are the least positive group of all, although those in senior roles are also less positive than average.

Case-study findings were broadly supportive. Most believed that the function now had equal standing with other professions within the organisation and was widely seen to be a good place to work. In part this transformation was due to HR having moved position from reactive and administrative to becoming more responsive and enabling. This transition was felt to be a major component of the renaissance of HR. These shifts were not only important to the outward persona of HR, but were also key to the job satisfaction and interest many HR employees perceived in their work. While the professionalisation of the function was seen to have been enormously positive, concerns were voiced over the profession making itself more impenetrable to entry from the line. Professional identity was important, but the connection with the business was vital, too, and the ability of people to move in and out of the function and to enhance the connection between HR and the business was of enormous value.

These concerns seemed to carry less weight in the survey. One of the purposes of the survey was to find out whether HR professionals had experience in other functions and, if so, which functions. Overall, 83 per cent of respondents have worked outside HR, and around half of these provided details of this work. The most frequently quoted function was sales/marketing/retail, cited by 17 per cent of those who gave details, followed by general business/general management (16 per cent), finance (16 per cent), administration (12 per cent), operations (seven per cent), IT (four per cent), engineering/design (four per cent), production (three per cent), customer services (three per cent), education/teaching (three per cent) and project/ product management/ quality (three per cent).

Where HR had been outsourced, positive views on professional standing tended to be more muted: the decision to outsource most of HR was seen to be indicative in itself of a perspective of HR where there is relatively little engagement with its strategic role. A contract relationship may make it more difficult to create mutual understanding, engagement and respect.

A professional qualification

Within the case studies, the move to become more professional in outlook has driven an increasing demand for professional qualifications. The need for qualified people relates to the ability to credibly deliver the role, to command respect and trust in judgement. It was also important for the self-regard of the profession. As we have mentioned previously, however, the qualification could be seen as a badge to gain entry rather than conveying a measurably different level of competence. For some roles, the qualification has less credibility in the marketplace – in consultancy particularly, experience is valued more. Some groups, such as OD specialists and some interviewees from local government, were critical of the qualification not catering for their needs.

'HR leaders see the need for both "hard" HR skills (quantitative analysis and business view) and a more ethical perspective on the employment relationship.'

Many commented on the need for further qualifications beyond the Professional Development Scheme (PDS), to provide a focus for a mid-career, advanced level development programme for those already in HR seeking a deeper, more challenging approach. It was suggested that such qualifications should be much more specialised.

Discussion on the CIPD qualification gave rise to other comments about the need to recognise both some of the wider qualifications in the marketplace, and also, through some kind of accreditation system, the learning contained in these. Many younger people felt there was a growth in new qualifications in which HR was a significant element, but these were not valued to the same extent in the marketplace.

A professional skill set

Not all our case studies had, as yet, paid much attention to the changing skill sets that new structures and ways of delivering HR demanded. Yet, where they had, they were clear on what the important attributes were.

The Prudential, for example, places considerable value on HR specialist expertise, reinforced by the service centre structure. At the more junior end, the service centre work needs mental agility. At higher levels, specific experience of the work area is required plus numerical and analytical skills. Getting good people in the reward field is especially difficult, as judgements need to be quite pragmatic and decisions also often need to be made quickly.

In the Prudential model, the more specialised roles in the service centres work with managers out in the business, so it is not a 'back-room' role. This business exposure is also seen as important

development for people working in specialist roles and enables them to move at a later stage into business partner or senior leadership roles in HR.

The business partner roles need relationship-building, influencing, and negotiating skills, plus professional skills and business understanding.

For a senior role in HR you need to develop several skill sets: first the nuts and bolts of HR – understanding technical aspects of the work; second the broader view of the business and the function and strategic and influencing skills; third an appreciation of the cultural and business context and which questions need to be asked.

HR leaders see the need for both 'hard' HR skills (quantitative analysis and business view) and a more ethical perspective on the employment relationship. Creativity is also needed to find fresh solutions to the tensions between the needs of the business and the needs of employees. The OD skill set is becoming more important: understanding the business and being trusted by managers. Our local authority case study commented that it was difficult finding people who could move into OD roles and had the ability to analyse and work with managers to provide solutions.

Those who had experienced senior generalist HR roles felt that they needed specialist expertise in the team reporting to them, especially in areas of HR in which they did not have particular expertise themselves.

At Cancer Research UK it was similarly felt that the more junior generalist roles, especially in the Service Centre, require inter-personal and problem-solving skills, but not necessarily much specific experience or knowledge – this is acquired on the job. Some staff performing these roles felt that attention to detail was important, having a patient

> 'The tensions between cost-cutting and strategic partnering have led to new structures that do not always sit comfortably alongside old models of HR and old career paths.'

manner and being able to prioritise tasks was important. In some areas, such as Resourcing, HR people have to be quite tough to stand up to managers who have strong opinions and enjoy rigorous intellectual debate on staffing matters, for example, senior research scientists. HR people need to be quick to pick up on the particular business needs and the culture – a skill set not always found when recruiting for HR people. This demand for professionals who can hold their own with professionals of a different discipline was also seen in Lovells – a law firm – and in Guy's and St Thomas'.

Central roles in development and training involve facilitation rather than direct delivery, which is often bought in from external providers. These advisory roles are not very easy to fill, and the quality of applicants for senior roles in learning and development was felt to be significantly affected by the salary offered.

Several participants – especially those in senior roles – felt that people aspiring to HR Director roles needed both practical experience and in-depth understanding of a number of fields within HR. Reward is seen as important, but not just in the narrow technical sense of pay systems, but also in the wider context of the overall employment relationship.

The future

It is a confusing time for HR, with pressures to become increasingly strategic and to create and manage new roles within the organisation. The tensions between cost-cutting and strategic partnering have led to new structures that do not always sit comfortably alongside old models of HR and old career paths. Even where structures seem, on the surface, to be quite traditional, the desire to have more qualified individuals in post and to

create a more interactive relationship with the line has changed roles significantly.

In one organisation, the desire to move to a business partner approach had caused confusion for staff. We had comments from HR advisers that they did not understand what would need to be different in their behaviour in order to become a business partner.

Shared services and outsourcing have led to dispersed HR units, dealing with their client base in a more remote and transactional way, while business partners seek to get closer to the organisation and make a strategic contribution. While many are grappling with the implications of these structures, others have commented on the need to ensure that the operational support role of HR still gets done. They felt it was important not to reduce the function into change agents when they were also there to provide stability and keep the organisation running effectively. The risk is that the operational focus for HR gets neglected in favour of the strategic.

Some things never change

But not everything changes; senior HR people believed that advisory-style roles would still be required in the future and would still need to draw on teams of experts in order to provide an integrated service to customers. The interplay between HR adviser and business partner is still being debated and business partners, too, need specialist support to call upon.

Many are optimistic about the function, seeing it as likely to provide a positive career in the future, because it remains at the heart of the business and because of the growing research that indicates that effective people-management practices can make significant contributions to business

> 'Despite concerns over some of the new roles and structures, many saw that they also provided the opportunity to get close to the line and make a contribution...'

performance. Despite concerns over some of the new roles and structures, many saw that they also provided the opportunity to get close to the line and make a contribution (this was echoed in the survey, too). Other organisations predicted staff cuts or raised a concern that the function could become complacent, ignoring the ever-present pressure to reduce costs and relaxing the drive to visibly demonstrate value. The survey also found that respondents are reasonably optimistic about HR's prospects as a provider of jobs in the years ahead, in that only around one-third feel that there will be fewer HR jobs in the future, or that their own organisation will need fewer HR practitioners. However, call centres are viewed less favourably, with under 20 per cent believing that they offer good career opportunities. Outsourcing is also a concern to some, in that almost 40 per cent feel it has impacted negatively on HR careers.

It was felt that HR practitioners may need to continue to move between generalist and specialist roles to acquire a rounded skill set and develop credibility. It was felt by some that certain of the current key roles, eg employee relations, may diminish in importance over time, as line managers acquire greater confidence and capability. In some organisations, however, (especially those in some parts of the public sector), where there are considerable numbers of grievances, disciplinary cases and Employment Tribunal applications to deal with, an employee relations role is still critical. Thus, it seems the content of the HR role will remain context-specific.

And some things are always changing...

At present, the traditional administrative entry route into HR looks like it is being replaced in the bigger, more complex organisations by one through Service Centre work, where individuals have the opportunity to develop a broad range of skills, from process management to supporting managers. This provides opportunities for those from very varied backgrounds, but they do not necessarily have smooth routes out to other parts of the community unless the company puts effort and resources into training and developing them.

Outsourcing relationships will undoubtedly evolve as different models of the client–supplier relationship are tried and tested. Currently, it can be rather transactional where the focus is on the contract rather than what it delivers and, in one of our case studies, there was a desire to move to something more strategic, working alongside managers to offer solutions to business problems.

Finally, ongoing changes in working style and practices also have implications for the development of HR professionals. Some of our case studies discussed the fact that greater flexibility in working practices (eg hotdesking; working from home etc) had created some unforeseen issues for learning and career development in the workplace. While these practices provide huge benefits in work–life management, some organisations had found that they can also make it difficult for new or young staff to form close working relationships with colleagues and gain access to informal learning and coaching.

8 | Emerging issues

What has emerged from this research is a range of potential tensions for the function which revolve around roles in HR and the consequent changing shape of HR careers.

New forms of HR

Underpinning these tensions is the fact that, in many organisations the function has fundamentally changed its interaction with the organisation and has sought to continue the drive to be more responsive and proactive. New forms of organisation, driven by a philosophy of greater consolidation, standardisation and automation and heavily influenced by the writings of Dave Ulrich have resulted in many HR functions seeking to shift their emphasis from administration and operational matters to strategic partnership and change management.

Nonetheless, administrative tasks still have to be done. As a result, there is a tendency to separate them from the rest of HR by locating them within shared services centres or outsourced providers. In some cases, this can lead to a marginalisation of administrative support and the people who provide it. However, some organisations have made considerable efforts to ensure that this does not take place through encouraging rotation of roles or buddying shared services staff with business partners or experts. Indeed, where effort is made, these administrative roles can provide a source of emerging talent. In smaller organisations, roles tend to be less segregated, which gives individuals wider opportunities.

Demarcations between transactional and 'transformational' activities have always existed, but are now more marked than ever. Similar traditional distinctions between specialists and generalists are also becoming more emphasised,

especially in the large organisations where there are centres of expertise (where the capability requirements have grown) and business partners.

These distinct HR communities can sometimes become quite separated in location, leadership, philosophy, aims and stakeholder interactions, and these divisions may mean that ideas, approaches, views and talent are not shared. The fact that skill requirements are also different from each other makes the task of developing people into these roles all the harder, especially since within the specialist community, areas like reward, employee relations, learning and development are growing apart with the deepening of expertise.

There is a related issue that in some organisations there seems to be an identity division between HR and training and OD functions. Depending on approach, this can then be carried into skills demanded and the kinds of people that are looked for to staff the function.

Just how has HR responded? From this research it would seem that the initial focus of the function has been on redesigning roles and structures in HR to reflect the three-legged model of Ulrich and others. Perhaps there has in fact been too much focus here and not enough attention paid to other aspects intimately connected to making a success of such structure and role changes. These complementary changes are to skills, processes and career paths. HR needs to pay more attention to these key areas if it is to nurture and retain talent. It may be that this is a matter of timing, and a focus on the people aspects of the organisational changes will come soon enough. However, it may be that, with so much activity elsewhere, there is a need for a timely reminder to remember the people caught up in all this change – an unusual message to have to deliver to HR.

'The function needs to think carefully about where new entrants fit and how they progress. Deliberate developmental roles for HR graduates and other entrants would be much welcomed.'

For those within the HR function the message is that, within some organisations and across the HR community as a whole, fragmented careers have arisen from the separation of service centres, centres of expertise and business partners. In future people will have to make 'zigzag' moves to gain both operational experience and close working with the business, plus real know-how in key sub-areas of HR.

Impact on entry

The brightest and best are finding HR a difficult nut to crack. Graduates are selecting HR as a potential career but then finding their experiences are not greatly valued in the marketplace, and the jobs that are available to them are very few and often dull. Getting in is bad enough, but moving on may be even more fraught. Entry-level jobs, designed as such and with progression and development opportunities built in, are rare indeed. It may be that the function is shooting itself in the foot, given the lack of good people, by designing difficult-to-fill jobs, such as the business partner. It requires incumbents to be able to think and act strategically in conjunction with more senior colleagues and in complex situations.

Preparation for such a role is by no means easy. Recruiting from the external market may be a short-term solution, but who is investing in the development of these individuals and how are they doing it? Clearly, a degree cannot fully prepare someone for an HR career. Thus, the professional qualification, and time to be fully inducted into the organisation and learn the ropes, are essential – the problem is that these crucial elements are often out of reach as well.

As we have seen, at the other end of the spectrum, traditional routes in from those keen on the administrative side of personnel are also less easy to access and many felt these were drying up.

The function needs to think carefully about where new entrants fit and how they progress. Deliberate developmental roles for HR graduates and other entrants would be much welcomed. Once entry is gained, the opportunity to study for relevant qualifications together with developmental experiences such as project roles, junior business partner roles alongside more senior colleagues, secondments, and deliberate job moves can all act as stepping stones to ongoing development.

Individuals interested in an HR career would do well to consider degree courses where CIPD qualifications are built in or where there is a strong emphasis on HR. Gaining work experience in an HR function, either during holiday periods or at the end of a degree, will also help position applications. Individuals might also want to consider working in the public sector, which is, on the whole, more amicable to providing initial developmental experience.

Of course, not everyone working in HR will spend their entire career in the function. It is a strength of HR that it can pull in people with other experiences in mid-career and also that HR professionals can work outside the function for periods of time, especially to gain line-management experience and business understanding. Career paths and structures for development need to be flexible in offering options for mid-career entrants as well as those who pursue the more conventional pattern of gaining professional skills and qualifications in HR in their twenties.

'HR functions need to think about how to develop career paths into and out of specialist roles and also consider instigating training for senior specialists.'

Impact on skills

New skills sets

Changing job roles means changing skills sets and there is a general view emerging from this research that some skill sets are hard to find. OD roles, where technical and consultancy knowledge, skills and experience are combined, are problematic to resource: people often have one skill set or the other, not both. Organisations also find business partner roles difficult to resource, which may imply that there is a career failure at this point in time. This is not surprising, as traditional HR hierarchies have not created enough people ready for this newly emerging career stream. We might expect that this is a blip in the system and that these skills shortages will resolve themselves over time as new career paths are formed, but there are indications that they may not.

As we have seen, the new forms of HR delivery lead to quite isolated populations, and younger people comment on the difficulty of making transitions. Both shared services and outsourced provision can act to limit the learning from clients and colleagues that would be commonplace in a more integrated community. This can inhibit the opportunities for people to acquire the skills they need to progress between roles, and it is only when organisations put processes in place to facilitate skills growth that it seems these barriers are likely to be overcome. We did see some excellent examples of organisations quite deliberately creating zigzag careers between shared services, specialists and business partners to enhance skill gains. This is essential, too, for corporate HR that is fed in career-stream terms from these lower-lying tributaries.

Creating these opportunities is difficult enough in an organisation which values the function, but not all organisations are ready or willing to engage in a strategic dialogue with HR; for some they conceptualise HR as about 'tea and sympathy', or cutting costs to the minimum. This means that *professional* credibility is often about *personal* credibility and the role of each member of staff in building this. It is sometimes difficult to find enough of these kinds of staff to feel confident about delivering the expressed promise.

Specialist skills

Some organisations commented on a difficulty in finding good specialists, and individuals we spoke to have also discussed the difficulties of career progression in specialist roles. The difficulty for individuals is that there are no easy choices. Some specialisms have relatively short career horizons and people fear being caught. There is a tendency, therefore, to alternate between generalist and specialist careers to acquire good breadth of experience and to ensure that a wide variety of potential job moves remain open. This is not to say that there are no attractions for specialists; for those not wanting to reach a director level appointment, and there are many who do not wish to do so, a senior specialist role can be very satisfying. The problem for HR is that, in the new HR structures, it is more difficult to see how specialists might be developed. This suggests that HR functions need to think about how to develop career paths into and out of specialist roles and also consider instigating training for senior specialists.

New skills

Structural and socio-economic change clearly impact on HR people. There was a recognition that HR can be a tough profession, and is becoming more so. HR professionals needed to offer a new range of skills and be able to operate in a sensitive, political and highly competitive business market, while demonstrating value. For example, for those supplying HR services or those managing the suppliers there is a requirement for well-developed commercial skills. Finding the right kinds of people and being able to reward, develop and progress them, is difficult for many HR functions.

High-level skills

At high level, careers lead to director-level roles and these people need wide experience and very strong business and influencing skills. Know-how across several of the broad areas of HR (eg employee relations, reward, learning and development, service centre operations) will be important for aspiring HR directors. There are, however, also more specialist careers in HR where deep know-how leads to high-level posts in employee development/OD and reward in particular.

Impact on relationships

The current predominant theory is to promote a climate of warm and engaged relationships between HR and the organisation. The emphasis is on strategic partnership, working with the line to deliver better value for the organisation and for employees. This has also been a significant driver of the other changes we have seen – professionalising the function in terms of qualifications and creating new roles embedded with the line. These relationships, however, do need to be nurtured, and yet some aspects of HR make this more difficult. The geographical location of HR functions, especially shared services, but also sometimes outsourced providers, can make creating and maintaining the relationships essential for work very difficult. Relationships work

better where people can access a face for advice, not just a voice or a screen.

Response of HR

What we have seen in response to skill gaps is that organisations have sought to fill them through external recruitment. Several of our case studies commented that they had found it difficult to promote their own staff into more responsible roles with internal candidates lacking the appropriate skills. However, several of our case studies have also commented that they have found it difficult to find appropriately skilled external candidates when advertising, and some mentioned that they resorted to appointing less-skilled internal candidates and intended to spend some time developing them. These individual fixes are clearly neither strategic nor a very efficient way of resolving such resourcing problems. These findings suggest a general shortage of skills or relevant experience in the HR labour market to which most organisations have not, as yet, thought through what their response should be.

It is clear that HR functions would benefit from spending more time thinking through the implications of new forms of HR for skills and consider proactive development activity to help people gain the skill sets they need. This might involve shaping roles differently, as Lovells have done, or creating buddying opportunities as in the Prudential.

What is emerging is a gap between the aspirations of the function to deliver certain roles and its ability to develop individuals into them. It is likely that quite active management of careers will emerge as being increasingly necessary if the moves from specialist to generalist and between the various parts of the HR community are to

'**... does the function practice what it preaches when it comes to the career development of its own people?**'

become a reality. Such sideways, or diagonal, moves need proactive management if they are to take place when people need them.

Effective career development and learning

The HR function usually holds responsibility for career development policy in the organisation and often works very closely with business managers and leaders to proactively develop talent and widen career opportunities for individuals. So, does the function practice what it preaches when it comes to the career development of its own people?

This study shows a very mixed picture. Many HR professionals will not expect to spend their whole career inside one organisation, but might reasonably expect to have some active career development while they remain. Overall career development was patchy, with the majority of case-study organisations feeling that they should have rather more systematic approaches to developing careers, but lacking these at present. Useful practices might include:

◘ Re-articulation of the kinds of roles needed in HR and kinds of career paths available. If competence frameworks are used in HR, they must keep pace with the change in the nature of HR work.

◘ The HR director playing a strong head-of-profession role for the people in the HR function, ensuring a positive approach to both skill and career development and systematically reviewing bench strength and development needs in the function.

◘ A more open approach to discussing career issues confidentially with individual employees

and helping them assess whether they can pursue their career further in the same organisation, if that is what they wish to do.

◘ Encouraging some movement between HR and other business functions. This should include opportunities for HR people to spend periods of time in roles outside the function or to undertake work with a very strong business focus. These experiences will be important in growing the next generation of strong HR generalists and business partners.

◘ Movement across specialisms within HR and between generalist roles (eg in service centres) and more specialist roles (eg in areas of expertise) will not happen easily without positive intervention. It can be achieved by job rotation or internal secondments as well as by formal job moves. Such experiences should be part of the PDP approach for people in HR and senior managers and directors within HR should be accountable for facilitating such moves.

◘ Informal approaches to learning should be augmented by structured early-career training, including support for professional study for those seeking to make a career in HR. Mentoring would seem especially appropriate for supporting careers and development in HR, and could be accommodated in smaller HR functions. HR staff should have access to both internal and external networks or communities of practice to extend relationships and engage in learning from other organisations.

The role of individuals

◘ Individuals, too, have a role to play and, undoubtedly in many functions, the onus on career development will be with the individual. Individuals therefore need to be willing to create and maximise their own career opportunities. Finding possible buddy partners, looking for secondment opportunities, and working with one's line manager to explore work-based development opportunities will all be helpful.

◩ Every individual should have a PDP agreed with their line manager and which explores formal and informal opportunities.

◩ Individuals should create their own networks with other professionals, both inside and outside their organisation. CIPD events can be very helpful here, as can conferences and professional support groups, such as local CIPD branches.

◩ A move outside the HR function will help broaden experience. Individuals will need to think carefully as to when this might be most appropriate and talk to senior people within the function about the possibilities of doing this as part of an explicit development process.

References

ARNOLD, J. (1997)

Managing Careers into the 21st Century. London: Paul Chapman.

ARTHUR, M. B. and ROUSSEAU, D. M. (EDS) (1996)

The Boundaryless Career: a New Employment Principle for a New Organisational Era. Oxford: Oxford University Press.

ATKINSON, J. and MEAGER, N. (1986)

Flexibility in Firms: A Study of Changing Working Patterns and Practices. Brighton: Institute for Manpower Studies.

BARBER, L., HILL, D., HIRSH, W. and TYERS, C. (2005)

Fishing for talent in a wider pool: Trends and Dilemmas in Corporate Graduate Recruitment. IES for IES/CIHE, Report 421. Brighton: Institute for Employment Studies.

BATES, S. (2001)

'No Experience Necessary?'. *HR Magazine.* November 2001.

BRADLEY, H., ERICKSON, M., STEPHENSON, C. and WILLIAMS, S. (2000)

Myths at Work. Cambridge: Polity Press.

BRIDGES, W. (1994)

Job shift: How to Prosper in a Workplace without Jobs. Reading MA: Addison-Wesley.

CARTER, A., HIRSH, W. and ASTON, J. (2002)

Resourcing the training and development function. IES Report 390, Brighton: Institute for Employment Studies.

CASTELLS, M. (1996)

The Rise of the Network Society. Oxford: Blackwell.

CHAMBERS, E., FOULON, M., HANDFIELD-JONES, H., HANKIN, S. M. and MICHAELS, E. D. (1998)

'The War for Talent'. *The McKinsey Quarterly,* No. 3, pp. 44–57.

CHARTERED INSTITUTE OF PERSONNEL AND DEVELOPMENT (2003)

Managing employee careers. Survey Report. London: CIPD.

CHARTERED INSTITUTE OF PERSONNEL AND DEVELOPMENT (2004)

The HR Survey: Where We Are, Where We're Heading. Survey Report. London: CIPD.

CHARTERED INSTITUTE OF PERSONNEL AND DEVELOPMENT (2005).

HR: Where is your career heading? Survey Report. London: CIPD.

COLLIN, A and WATTS, A. G. (1996)

'The Death and Transfiguration of Career – and of career guidance?' *British Journal of Guidance and Counselling,* 24(3), pp. 385–398.

DALTON, G. (1989)

'Developmental Views of Careers in Organisations'. In Arthur, M. B., Hall, D. T. and Lawrence, B. S. (eds), *Handbook of Career Theory.* Cambridge: Cambridge University Press.

DALTON, G., THOMPSON, P. and PRICE, P. (1977)

'The Four Stages of Professional Careers'. In *Organisational Dynamics.* Vol. 6, No. 23, pp. 19–42.

FELSTEAD, A., KRAHN, H. and POWELL, M. (1999)

'Young and Old at Risk: Comparative Trends in "Non-standard" Patterns of Employment in Canada and the United Kingdom'. *International Journal of Manpower,* 20(5), pp. 277–296.

GRADY, D. and FINEHAM, T. (1990)

'Making R & D pay'. *The McKinsey Quarterly,* No. 3, pp. 161–175.

GREGG, P. and WADSWORTH, J. (1999)

'"Job Tenure", 1975–98'. In Gregg, P. and Wadsworth, J. (eds), *The State of Working Britain.* pp.109–126, Manchester: Manchester University Press.

HANDY, C. (1994)

The Empty Raincoat. London: Hutchinson.

HIRSH, W. (2003)

'Positive Career Development for Leaders and Managers'. In *Leadership in Organizations: Current issues and key trends.* Edited by John Storey, Routledge.

HIRSH, W. and JACKSON, C. (2004)

Managing Careers in Large Organisations. Work Foundation.

HOPPE, M. H. (1993)

'The Effects of National Culture on the Theory and Practice of Managing R & D Professionals Abroad'. *R&D Management.* Vol. 23, No. 4, pp. 313–325.

IRS EMPLOYMENT REVIEW (2004)

HR Careers Survey. Employment Trends, December.

JARVIS, P. (2003)

Career Management Paradigm Shift: Prosperity for citizens, windfall for governments. Ottawa: National Life/Work Centre (mimeo).

KANTER, R. M. (1989)

When Giants Learn to Dance. New York: Simon & Schuster.

LAMBERT, A. (2002)

Careers in HR and Other Support Functions. Careers Research Forum.

LAWLER, E. and MOHRMAN, S. A. (2003)

'HR as a Strategic Partner'. *Human Resource Planning.* Vol. 26, No. 3.

LAWLER, E., MUELLER-OERLINGHAUSEN, J. and SHEARN, J. A. (2005)

'A Dearth of HR Talent'. *McKinsey Quarterly.* No. 2.

MACAULEY, C. (2003)

'Job Mobility and Job Tenure in the UK'. *Labour Market Trends*. 111(11), pp. 541–550.

MCKENNA, P. and MAISTER, D. (2002)

First Among Equals. New York: Free Press.

NICHOLSON, N. and WEST, M. (1988)

Managerial Job Change: Men and Women in Transition. Cambridge: Cambridge University Press.

NOLAN, P. (2003)

'Reconnecting with History: the ESRC Future of Work Programme'. *Work, Employment and Society*. 17(3), pp. 473–480.

PURCELL, J., KINNIE, N., HUTCHINSON, S., RAYTON, B. and SWART, J. (2003)

Understanding the People and Performance Link: Unlocking the Black Box. London: CIPD.

REILLY, P. and WILLIAMS, T. (2003)

How to Get Best Value From HR: The Shared Services Option. Aldershot: Gower.

REILLY, P. and WILLIAMS, T. (FORTHCOMING)

Strategic HR: Building HR Capability. Aldershot: Gower.

SUFF, P. and REILLY, P. (2005)

'In the Know: Reward and Performance Management of Knowledge Workers'. Brighton: Institute for Employment Studies. www.employment-studies.co.uk

SWART, J. and KINNIE, N. (2004)

Managing the Careers of Professional Knowledge Workers. London: CIPD.

TAYLOR, R. (2004)

'Britain's Work of Work – Myths and Realities'. London: ESRC.

TORRINGTON, D. (1998)

'Crisis and Opportunity in HRM: the Challenge for the Personnel Function'. In Sparrow. P. and Marchington, M. (eds), *Human Resource Management: The New Agenda*. London: Pitman Financial Times.

TRADES UNION CONGRESS (2000)

The Future of Work. London: TUC.

ULRICH, D. (1995)

'Shared Services: From Vogue to Value'. *Human Resource Planning*. Vol. 18, (3), pp. 12–23.

WATERMAN, R., WATERMAN, J. and COLLARD, B. (1994)

'Towards a Career Resilient Workforce'. *Harvard Business Review*. July–August.

WEEKES, S. (2005)

'Hop To It'. Special Report: Careers, *Personnel Today*. January 18th 2005.

WEIR, G .(2003)

'Self-employment in the UK Labour Market'. *Labour Market Trends*. 111(9), pp. 441–451.

WHITE, M., HILL, S., MILLS, C. and SMEATON, D. (2004,)

Managing to Change? Basingstoke: Palgrave Macmillan.